BE
JOYFUL

BE

JOYFUL

EVEN WHEN THINGS GO WRONG, YOU CAN HAVE JOY

NT COMMENTARY

PHILIPPIANS

Warren W. Wiersbe

David C Cook®
transforming lives together

BE JOYFUL
Published by David C Cook
4050 Lee Vance View
Colorado Springs, CO 80918 U.S.A.

David C Cook Distribution Canada
55 Woodslee Avenue, Paris, Ontario, Canada N3L 3E5

David C Cook U.K., Kingsway Communications
Eastbourne, East Sussex BN23 6NT, England

The graphic circle C logo is a registered trademark of David C Cook.

LCCN 2008924752
ISBN 978-1-4347-6846-9
eISBN 978-1-4347-6592-5

First edition of *Be Joyful* by Warren W. Wiersbe published by Victor Books®
in 1974 © Warren W. Wiersbe, ISBN 0-89693-739-9

The Team: Gudmund Lee, Amy Kiechlin, Jack Campbell, and Susan Vannaman
Series Cover Design: John Hamilton Design
Cover Photo: iStockPhoto

Printed in the United States of America
Second Edition 2008

12 13 14 15 16 17

091015

Dedicated to
Wayne Christianson,
whose friendship I appreciate, and
whose journalistic skill I admire

CONTENTS

THE BIG IDEA

An Introduction to *Be Joyful*
by Ken Baugh

Joy leaks. Have you ever noticed that? One minute you can be on top of the world, and the next minute in the pit of despair. To hold on to a joyful state of mind seems as pointless as trying to carry water in a holy bucket—it might work for a moment, but that is hardly enough. And yet the Bible exhorts us to "be joyful *always*" (1 Thess. 5:16 NIV). Most of us think that's impossible, though—just another one of those "suggestions" from the Bible that doesn't make sense in real life. But being joyful wasn't impossible for the apostle Paul. He seemed to be able to live his life in a perpetual state of joy, and he wanted to help others live in that joy too.

The book of Philippians is Paul's personal manifesto on how to live a life full of joy. We see this over and over again throughout the letter: "I always pray with joy …" (1:4 NIV); "I rejoice …" (1:18 NIV); "I will continue to rejoice …" (1:18 NIV); "be glad and rejoice with me" (2:18 NIV); "rejoice in the Lord!" (3:1 NIV); "Rejoice in the Lord always" (4:4 NIV). And on and on it goes, chapter after chapter the word *joy* drips off every page in various forms. It makes a thinking person wonder, *How did Paul do it? How did Paul live in a constant state of joy?* Was he some kind of super-saint with a faith made of different stuff than the rest of us? Did he live in a constant state of denial? Or did he live such a problem-free life that to be sad, depressed, or in despair never occurred to him?

Well, if there is one thing that is true about the apostle Paul, it is that his life was not easy. Paul lived almost every day of his life in mortal danger and physical pain. In 2 Corinthians 11:23–27 (MSG), Paul sums up the harsh realities of his life as an apostle:

> I've worked much harder, been jailed more often, beaten up more times than I can count, and at death's door time after time. I've been flogged five times with the Jews' thirty-nine lashes, beaten by Roman rods three times, pummeled with rocks once. I've been shipwrecked three times, and immersed in the open sea for a night and a day. In hard traveling year in and year out, I've had to ford rivers, fend off robbers, struggle with friends, struggle with foes. I've been at risk in the city, at risk in the country, endangered by desert sun and sea storm, and betrayed by those I thought were my brothers. I've known drudgery and hard labor, many a long and lonely night without sleep, many a missed meal, blasted by the cold, naked to the weather.

As if these things were not enough, Paul also suffered from some type of physical ailment that he called a "thorn in the flesh," which tormented him every day of his life (2 Cor. 12:7 NIV). Finally, according to church history, Emperor Nero killed Paul by cutting off his head sometime around AD 67. Needless to say, despite what some might say about the apostle Paul, he clearly did not live a charmed life. So then here is my question: What was the secret to Paul's joy?

In spite of his incredible hardships and daily physical suffering, how was he able to maintain a continual state of joy? How was he able to say to the Philippians, "Be glad and rejoice with me" (2:18 NIV)?

Well, I won't disclose to you all of Paul's secrets right now—for those you need to have your Bible in one hand and Wiersbe's commentary in the other. But I will give you a hint: I believe that Paul's ability to be joyful was due to the *source* of his joy. Three different times in his letter to the Philippians Paul revealed that his joy was "*in* the Lord" (3:1, 4:4, 4:10 NIV) rather than in the difficult, painful, constantly changing circumstances of life. But what does that mean? Simply this: To find joy we must place our confidence and hope in the character and nature of God. For Paul, this happened in two ways.

First, Paul was able to have joy because of his confidence in the sovereignty of God. You see, Paul believed that no matter what happened to him, God was in control of his life; and God never falls asleep at the wheel. For instance, in Philippians 1:12–18 (NIV) we discover that Paul is in prison as he writes this letter, but he is not discouraged by this. Instead he sees his chains as part of God's sovereign plan to encourage others in their proclamation of the gospel. Look at what he says: "Because of my chains, most of the brothers in the Lord have been encouraged to speak the word of God more courageously and fearlessly." Because Paul was able to see his chains from the perspective of God's sovereignty, he was able to rejoice. He didn't view his imprisonment as an interruption in his work to proclaim the gospel, rather he saw it all playing out according to God's sovereign plan. You see, when we trust that God is in control of all things—the good, the bad, and the ugly—we can be joyful because we know that God is working behind the scenes for our good and His glory.

Second, Paul was able to have joy because of his hope in heaven. God had given Paul a clear vision of heaven (2 Cor. 12:1–10), and this vision gave him incredible hope for the future that enabled him not only to press on throughout all the difficult circumstances of his life, but to do so with joy! "I press on toward the goal to win the prize for which God has called me heavenward in Christ Jesus" (Phil. 3:14 NIV). Paul's hope was in God's promise of heaven and God always keeps His promises. In fact, Paul was so encouraged by the reality of heaven that he considered all the troubles in this life to be small potatoes: "These hard times are *small potatoes* compared to the coming good times, the lavish celebration prepared for us" (2 Cor. 4:17 MSG). Never forget that life in this world is not all there is—we live seventy to ninety years at best on this planet, and many of those days are long and difficult, filled with pain and sorrow. But there is a new order of things coming where there will be no more death, no more sorrow, no more pain or suffering of any kind (Rev. 21:4). There is a lavish celebration awaiting us, where one day we will all sit and share a feast at God's table! Paul's confidence and hope "in the Lord" enabled him to live every day of his life filled with joy, and by the grace of God, it will enable you to do the same.

I am excited for you as you continue to uncover the secrets of Paul's ability to live a life filled with joy.

***

Dr. Wiersbe's commentaries have been a source of guidance and strength to me over the many years that I have been a pastor. His unique style is not overly academic, but theologically sound. He explains the deep truths of Scripture in a way that everyone can understand and apply. Whether you're a Bible scholar or a brand-new believer in Christ, you will benefit, as I have, from Warren's insights. With your Bible in one hand and Dr. Wiersbe's commentary in the other, you will be able to accurately unpack the deep truths of God's Word and learn how to apply them to your life.

Drink deeply, my friend, of the truths of God's Word, for in them you will find Jesus Christ, and there is freedom, peace, assurance, and joy.

—Ken Baugh
Pastor of Coast Hills Community Church
Aliso Viejo, California

A WORD FROM THE AUTHOR

Philippians is a joyful letter!

If you master the truths in Philippians, you should be filled with joy as you live the Christian life!

This little epistle from a Roman prisoner has grown on me over the years. I have preached it and taught it in churches and conferences across the country, and each time I come to it, the message is more real and exciting. My prayer is that it will become real and exciting to you.

As far as I know, this approach to Philippians is my own, although just about everybody who writes on the book deals with the subject of "joy" in one way or another. I first presented this material at Winona Lake, Indiana, in July 1961, and the outline was copyrighted in 1965. So many people have told me that the series has helped them that I'm encouraged to put it into print.

In spite of a busy schedule with many demands, it was a real joy to write this book. My prayer is that you might experience Christ's joy in your everyday life as you grasp the spiritual principles in Philippians.

—Warren W. Wiersbe

A Suggested Outline of the Book of Philippians

Theme: The joy of the Lord
Theme verse: Philippians 3:1

I. The Single Mind (Philippians 1)
  A. The fellowship of the gospel (Philippians 1:1–11)
  B. The furtherance of the gospel (Philippians 1:12–26)
  C. The faith of the gospel (Philippians 1:27–30)
II. The Submissive Mind (Philippians 2)
  A. The example of Christ (Philippians 2:1–11)
  B. The example of Paul (Philippians 2:12–18)
  C. The example of Timothy (Philippians 2:19–24)
  D. The example of Epaphroditus (Philippians 2:25–30)
III. The Spiritual Mind (Philippians 3)
  A. Paul's past—the accountant: "I count" (Philippians 3:1–11)
  B. Paul's present—the athlete: "I press" (Philippians 3:12–16)
  C. Paul's future—the alien: "I look" (Philippians 3:17–21)
IV. The Secure Mind (Philippians 4)
  A. God's peace (Philippians 4:1–9)
  B. God's power (Philippians 4:10–13)
  C. God's provision (Philippians 4:14–23)

Chapter One

9-3-

THE JOY-STEALERS

Mark Twain was a professional humorist whose lectures and writings made people around the world laugh and, for a short time, forget their troubles. Yet Mark Twain himself was, in private, a man whose life was broken by sorrow. When his beloved daughter Jean died suddenly of an epileptic seizure, Twain, too ill to go to the funeral, said to a friend, "I have never greatly envied anyone but the dead. 1 always envy the dead."

Jesus Christ was "a man of sorrows, and acquainted with grief." Yet He possessed a deep joy that was beyond anything the world could offer. As He faced the cruel death of Calvary, Jesus said to His followers, "These things have I spoken unto you, that my joy might remain in you, and that your joy might be full" (John 15:11).

Those who have trusted Christ have the privilege of experiencing "fulness of joy" (Ps. 16:11). Yet few Christians take advantage of this privilege. They live under a cloud of disappointment when they could be walking in the sunshine of joy. What has robbed them of their joy?

The answer to that important question is found in a letter written centuries ago. It was written by the apostle Paul when he was a prisoner in Rome about AD 62, and it was sent to his fellow Christians at the church in Philippi, a church Paul had founded on his second missionary journey (Acts 16). One of their members, Epaphroditus, had been sent to Rome to bring a special offering to the apostle and to help him in his time of difficulty (Phil. 2:25–30; 4:10–20). Paul's letter to the Philippian church is something of a missionary thank-you letter, but it is much more than that. It is the sharing of Paul's secret of Christian joy! At least nineteen times in these four chapters, Paul mentions joy, rejoicing, or gladness.

The unusual thing about the letter is this: Paul's situation was such that there appeared to be no reason for him to be rejoicing. He was a Roman prisoner, and his case was coming up shortly. He might be acquitted, or he might be beheaded! Acts 28:30–31 indicates that he was a prisoner in his own hired house, but he was chained to a Roman soldier and not permitted to preach in public. Paul had wanted to go to Rome as a preacher (Rom. 1:13–16); instead, he arrived as a prisoner. And, unfortunately, the believers at Rome were divided: Some were for Paul and some were against him (Phil. 1:15–17). In fact, some of the Christians even wanted to make things more difficult for the apostle!

Yet, in spite of his danger and discomfort, Paul overflowed with joy. What was the secret of this joy? The secret is found in another word that is often repeated in Philippians: It is the word *mind*. Paul uses *mind* ten times, and also uses the word *think* five times. Add the time he uses *remember* and you have a total of sixteen references to the mind. In other words, the secret of Christian joy is found in the way the believer thinks—his attitudes. After all, outlook determines outcome. As we think, so we are (Prov. 23:7). Philippians, then, is a Christian psychology book, based solidly on Bible doctrine. It is not a shallow self-help book that tells the reader how to convince himself that "everything is going to turn out all right." It is a book that explains the mind the believer must have if he is going to experience Christian joy in a world filled with trouble.

The best way to get the total picture of the book is to discover first the "thieves" that rob us of our joy, then determine the kinds of attitudes we must have in order to capture and conquer these thieves.

THE THIEVES THAT ROB YOU OF YOUR JOY

Circumstances. Most of us must confess that when things are going our way, we feel a lot happier and we are much easier to live with. "Dad must have had an easy day at the office," little Peggy said to her visiting girlfriend. "He didn't squeal the tires when he pulled into the driveway, and he didn't slam the door when he came into the house. And he even gave Mother a kiss!"

But have you ever stopped to consider how few of the circumstances of life are really under our control? We have no control over the weather or over the traffic on the expressway or over the things other people say and do. The person whose happiness depends on ideal circumstances is going to be miserable much of the time. The poet Byron wrote, "Men are the sport of circumstances." And yet here is the apostle Paul in the worst of circumstances, writing a letter saturated with joy!

People. My daughter jumped off the school bus as it stopped in front of our house and slammed her way through the front door. She marched defiantly up the stairs into her room and again slammed the door. All the time she was muttering under her breath, "People-people-*people*-PEOPLE!"

I went to her door and knocked softly. "May I come in?"

She replied, "No!"

I tried again, but she said it even more belligerently: "NO!"

I asked, "Why can't I come in?"

Her answer: "Because you're a people!"

All of us have lost our joy because of people: what they are, what they say, and what they do. (And no doubt we ourselves have contributed to making somebody else unhappy. It works both ways.) But we have to live and work with people; we cannot isolate ourselves and still live to glorify Christ. We are the light of the world and the salt of the earth. But sometimes the light grows dim and the salt becomes bitter because of other people. Is there any way to have joy in spite of people?

Things. A wealthy man was moving into his mansion, and his Quaker neighbor, who believed in simplicity of life, was watching the activities carefully. The neighbor counted the number of chairs and tables and the vast amount of bric-a-brac that was being carried into the house. Finally, he said to the lord of the mansion: "Neighbor, if thou dost need anything, come to see me and I will tell thee *how to get along without it!*"

Abraham Lincoln was walking down the street with his two sons, who were crying and fighting. "What's the matter with the boys?" a friend asked.

"The same thing that's wrong with the whole world," Lincoln replied. "I have three walnuts and each of the boys wants two."

Things! What thieves they can be. Yet Jesus said, "A man's life consisteth not in the abundance of the things which he possesseth" (Luke 12:15). In the Sermon on the Mount, Jesus warned against laying up treasures on earth: They are not safe, they do not last, and they never satisfy. Yet most people today think that joy comes from the things that they own. In reality, things can rob us of the only kind of joy that really lasts.

Worry. This is the worst thief of all. How many people have been robbed of peace and fulfillment because of worry? In fact, worry even has *physical* consequences, and while medicine can remove the symptoms, it cannot remove the cause. Worry is an "inside job." You can purchase sleep at the drug store, but you cannot purchase rest.

If Paul had wanted to worry, he had plenty of occasion. He was a political prisoner facing possible execution. His friends in Rome were divided in their attitudes toward his case. He had no mission board supporting him and no Legal Aid Society defending him. But in spite of all these difficulties, *Paul does not worry*! Instead, he writes a letter filled with joy and tells us how to stop worrying.

These, then, are the four thieves that rob us of joy: circumstances, people, things, and worry. How do we capture these thieves and keep them from taking away the joy that is rightfully ours in Christ? The answer is: *We must cultivate the right kind of mind.* If outlook determines outcome, then the attitude of mind that we cultivate will determine our joy or lack of it. In the four chapters of Philippians, Paul describes four attitudes of mind that will produce joy in spite of circumstances, people, and things, and that will keep us from worrying.

THE FOUR ATTITUDES THAT MAINTAIN YOUR JOY

(1) The Single Mind (Phil. 1). "A double minded man is unstable in all his ways" (James 1:8). Or, to use the old Latin proverb:

"When the pilot does not know what port he is heading for, no wind is the right wind." The reason many Christians are upset by circumstances is because they do not cultivate the single mind. Paul expresses this attitude of single-hearted devotion to Christ thus: "For to me to live is Christ, and to die is gain" (1:21).

In chapter 1, Paul discusses his difficult circumstances and faces them honestly. But his circumstances cannot rob him of his joy because he is not living to enjoy circumstances; he is living to serve Jesus Christ. He is a man with purpose: "This one thing I do" (3:13). He does not look at circumstances in themselves, but rather in relationship to Jesus Christ. He is not the prisoner of Rome; he is "the prisoner of Jesus Christ" (Eph. 3:1). The chains he wears are "my bonds in Christ" (Phil. 1:13). He is not facing a civil trial; he is "set for the defence of the Gospel" (1:17). He did not look at Christ through his circumstances; rather, he looked at his circumstances through Christ—and this changed everything.

When a Christian is single-minded, he is concerned about the *fellowship of the gospel* (1:1–11), the *furtherance of the gospel* (1:12–26), and the *faith of the gospel* (1:27–30). Paul rejoiced in his difficult circumstances because they helped to strengthen his fellowship with other Christians, gave him opportunity to lead others to Christ, and enabled him to defend the gospel before the courts of Rome. When you have the single mind, your circumstances work *for* you and not *against* you.

(2) The Submissive Mind (Phil. 2). This chapter focuses on *people*, and the key verse says, "Let nothing be done through strife or vainglory; but in lowliness of mind let each esteem other better [more important] than themselves" (v. 3). In chapter 1, Paul puts Christ first. In this chapter, he puts others second. Which means he puts himself last! The reason people aggravate us so much is usually because we do not have our own way. If we go through life putting *ourselves* first, and others go through life putting *themselves* first, then at many points there are going to be terrific battles.

A mother and her little son got on an elevator to go to the doctor's office. At the second floor a group of people got on, among them a rather large woman. As the elevator sped upward, the quiet was broken by a scream from the lips of the plump passenger. She turned to the mother and said, "Your son just bit me!"

The mother was horrified, but the little boy had an explanation: "She sitted in my face and I bited her!"

What took place on that elevator is taking place all over the world: People and nations bite each other because they get sat on or crowded.

But the Christian with the submissive mind does not expect others to serve him; he serves others. He considers the good of others to be more important than his own plans and desires. In chapter 2 we find four wonderful examples of the submissive mind: Jesus Christ (2:1–11), Paul (2:12–18), Timothy (2:19–24), and Epaphroditus (2:25–30). Each of these examples proves the principle, "For whosoever exalteth himself shall be abased; and he that humbleth himself shall be exalted" (Luke 14:11).

(3) The Spiritual Mind (Phil. 3). Eleven times in this chapter you find Paul using the word *things*. He points out that most people "mind earthly things" (v. 19), but that the spiritually minded Christian is concerned about heavenly things. "For our conversation [citizenship] is in heaven; from whence also we look for the Saviour, the Lord Jesus Christ" (v. 20). The person with the spiritual mind looks at the things of this world from heaven's point of view—and what a difference that makes!

When five missionaries were martyred by the Aucas in Ecuador, some newspapers and magazines considered the tragedy to be a great waste of life. While it did bring sorrow and grief to friends and loved ones, subsequent events proved that their deaths were not "waste" either for them or for the world. The words of Jim Elliot were true: "He is no fool who gives what he cannot keep to gain what he cannot lose."

The quest for things is robbing people of joy, and this includes Christian people. We want to possess things, and then we discover that things possess us. The only way to victory and joy is to have the spiritual mind and to look at things from God's point of view. Like Paul, we must be *accountants* with the right *values* (3:1–11), *athletes* with the right vigor (3:12–16), and *aliens* with the right *vision* (3:17–21). "I count … I press … I look" are the verbs that describe the person with the spiritual mind.

(4) The Secure Mind (Phil. 4). Worry is actually wrong thinking (the mind) and wrong feeling (the heart) about circumstances, people, and things. So if we have the single mind, the submissive mind, and the spiritual mind, we should not have too much trouble with worry. All we need is something to *guard* the heart and mind so that worry will not enter. Paul describes *the secure mind:* "And the peace of God, which passeth all understanding, shall keep your hearts and minds through Christ Jesus" (v. 7). That word *keep* is a military term; it means "stand guard, garrison." (Paul was chained to a soldier, you will remember.)

Chapter 4 describes the spiritual resources the believer has in Christ: God's peace (4:1–9), God's power (4:10–13), and God's provision (4:14–23). With resources like these, why should we worry? We have the peace of God to guard us (v. 7) and the God of peace to guide us (v. 9). The peace of God comes to us when we practice right praying (vv. 6–7), right thinking (v. 8), and right living (v. 9). This is God's secret for victory over all worry.

WHAT SHOULD WE DO?

This rapid survey of Philippians ought to convince us that it is possible to live a life of Christian joy in spite of circumstances, people, and things, and that we need not worry when the going is difficult. But how can we put all of this into practice in our lives? Here are four principles to help you remember these truths.

(1) Be sure you are a Christian. Paul wrote this letter to "all the saints in Christ Jesus" (1:1). That word *saint* simply means "a set-apart one." When you give yourself to Christ, you no longer belong to this world; you belong to Him and have been set apart for His glory. Each chapter in Philippians begins with either "in Christ" or "in the Lord" (1:1; 2:1; 3:1; 4:1). You cannot have the *single mind* ("For to me to live is Christ"—1:21), or the *submissive mind* ("Let each esteem other better than themselves"—2:3), or the *spiritual mind* ("For our conversation is in heaven"—3:20), or the secure mind ("And the peace of God ... shall keep your hearts and minds"—4:7) unless you belong to Jesus Christ. How does one become a child of God? Paul answered that question when he was in the Philippian jail: "Believe on the Lord Jesus Christ, and thou shalt be saved" (read Acts 16:6–40 for the whole story).

(2) Admit your failures. If we have been double-minded, proud, worldly minded, and filled with worry—*then we are sinning!* And the sooner we confess it to God, the sooner His joy will fill our lives. (Some people are actually proud of the fact that they worry, in spite of what Jesus says in Matthew 6:24–34.)

(3) Surrender your mind to Christ daily. Ask Him to give you a single mind, a submissive mind, a spiritual mind, and a secure mind. (In the chapters that follow, we will explain the way each of these minds functions in the Christian life.) When you find yourself losing your joy during the day, take inventory: "Do I have a double mind? Have I been proud? Am I grasping for things? Am I worrying?" If guilty, confess your sin then and there, and ask God to restore your mind as it ought to be.

(4) Look for opportunities to put your mind to work. If you really want a single mind, you can be sure the Lord will arrange circumstances so that you can begin to practice. "I told the Lord that I wanted Philippians 1:21 to work in my life," a new Christian told her pastor, "and guess what happened? I ended up in the hospital!"

The pastor asked, "Did you then look for opportunities to further the gospel, the way Paul did in Rome?"

Her face clouded. "No, I guess I didn't. I spent most of my time complaining."

You will discover during this study that God will give you regular "exams" in your daily life, to help you develop your spiritual attitudes. Learning and living go together, and He will give you the grace you need for every demand. As you practice exercising the right kind of attitude, you will find a deep joy welling up in your heart—joy in spite of circumstances, people, and things—and joy that defeats worry and fills you with the peace of God.

"But the fruit of the Spirit is love, joy, peace" (Gal. 5:22). Start letting this fruit grow in your life.

QUESTIONS FOR PERSONAL REFLECTION
OR GROUP DISCUSSION

1. Only true believers in Christ can experience the fullness of joy. What does "fullness of joy" mean to you? *Like A BABY (w) A WARM BoTTle A RATTle*

2. Why did Paul seem to be an unlikely person to write about joy? *Because he had been through so much persecution, beatings, STARVATION, He was beated*

3. What circumstances in your everyday life rob you of your Christian joy?

4. Are there certain people who irritate you without even trying? What can you do about that? *Yes: Just tell them I Love them*

5. Do you think Christians today are more or less concerned about things than Christians fifty years ago were? *Yes. I remember 50 years Ago i THings were Simpler.*

6. Do you worry often? What do you worry about?

7. What do you think it means to be single-minded? How can you better pursue this in your own life?

8. Do you find it hard to be submissive to other people? Why or why not?
(Some)

9. Do you consider yourself a spiritually minded person? Why or why not?

10. In what ways do you feel secure? In your job? In your family? In your relationship with Christ? Thank the Lord for these things before you continue.

Chapter Two

How to Increase Your Joy

(Philippians 1:1–11)

H ow about coming over to the house for some fellowship?"
"What a golf game! Man, did we have great fellowship!"
"The fellowship at the retreat was just terrific!"

That word *fellowship* seems to mean many things to many different people. Perhaps, like a worn coin, it may be losing its true impression. If so, we had better take some steps to rescue it. After all, a good Bible word like *fellowship* needs to stay in circulation as long as possible.

In spite of his difficult circumstances as a prisoner in Rome, Paul was rejoicing. The secret of his joy was the *single mind;* he lived for Christ and the gospel. (Christ is named eighteen times in Philippians 1, and the gospel is mentioned six times.) "For to me to live is Christ, and to die is gain" (Phil. 1:21). But what really is "the single mind"? It is the attitude that says, "It makes no difference what happens to me, just as long as Christ is glorified and the gospel shared with others." Paul rejoiced in spite of his circumstances, because his circumstances strengthened the *fellowship of the gospel* (Phil. 1:1–11), promoted *the furtherance of the gospel* (Phil. 1:12–26), and guarded *the faith of the gospel* (Phil. 1:27–30).

The word *fellowship* simply means "to have in common." But true

Christian fellowship is really much deeper than sharing coffee and pie, or even enjoying a golf game together. Too often what we think is fellowship is really only acquaintanceship or friendship. You cannot have fellowship with someone unless you have something in common, and for Christian fellowship, this means the possessing of eternal life within the heart. Unless a person has trusted Christ as his Savior, he knows nothing of "the fellowship of the gospel." In Philippians 2:1, Paul wrote about "the fellowship of the Spirit," because when a person is born again he receives the gift of the Spirit (Rom. 8:9). There is also "the fellowship of his sufferings" (Phil. 3:10). When we share what we have with others, this is also fellowship (Phil. 4:15, translated "communicate" in KJV).

So true Christian fellowship is much more than having a name on a church roll or being present at a meeting. It is possible to be close to people physically and miles away from them spiritually. One of the sources of Christian joy is this fellowship that believers have in Jesus Christ. Paul was in Rome, his friends were miles away in Philippi, but their spiritual fellowship was real and satisfying. When you have the single mind, you will not complain about circumstances because you know that difficult circumstances will result in the strengthening of the fellowship of the gospel.

Paul used three thoughts in Philippians 1:1–11 that describe true Christian fellowship: I have you in my mind (Phil. 1:3–6), I have you in my heart (Phil. 1:7–8), and I have you in my prayers (Phil. 1:9–11).

I HAVE YOU IN MY MIND (1:3–6)

Isn't it remarkable that Paul was thinking of others and not of himself? As he awaited his trial in Rome, Paul's mind went back to the believers in Philippi, and every recollection he had brought him joy. Read Acts 16; you may discover that some things happened to Paul at Philippi, the memory of which could produce sorrow. He was illegally arrested and beaten, was placed in the stocks, and was humiliated before the people. But even those memories brought joy to Paul, because it was through this suffering that the jailer found Christ! Paul recalled Lydia and her household, the poor slave girl who had been demon possessed, and the other dear Christians at Philippi, and each recollection was a source of joy. (It is worth asking, "Am I the kind of Christian who brings joy to my pastor's mind when he thinks of me?")

It is possible that Philippians 1:5 is talking about their *financial* fellowship with Paul, a topic he picks up again in Philippians 4:14–19. The church at Philippi was the only church that entered into fellowship with Paul to help support his ministry. The "good work" of Philippians 1:6 may refer to the sharing of their means; it was started by the Lord, and Paul was sure the Lord would continue it and complete it.

But we will not go astray if we apply these verses to the work of salvation and Christian living. We are not saved by our good works (Eph. 2:8–9). Salvation is the good work God does in us when we trust His Son. In Philippians 2:12–13 we are told that God continues to work in us through His Spirit. In other words, salvation includes a threefold work:

1. the work God does *for* us—salvation;
2. the work God does *in* us—sanctification;
3. the work God does *through* us—service.

This work will continue until we see Christ, and then the work will be fulfilled. "We shall be like him; for we shall see him as he is" (1 John 3:2).

It was a source of joy to Paul to know that God was still working in the lives of his fellow believers at Philippi. After all, this is the real basis for joyful Christian fellowship, to have God at work in our lives day by day.

"There seems to be friction in our home," a concerned wife said to a marriage counselor. "I really don't know what the trouble is."

"Friction is caused by one of two things," said the counselor, and to illustrate he picked up two blocks of wood from his desk. "If one block is moving and one is standing still, there's friction. Or if both are moving but in opposite directions, there's friction. Now, which is it?"

"I'll have to admit that I've been going backward in my Christian life, and Joe has really been growing," the wife admitted. "What I need is to get back to fellowship with the Lord."

I HAVE YOU IN MY HEART (1:7–8)

Now we move a bit deeper, for it is possible to have others in our minds without really having them in our hearts. (Someone has observed that many people today would have to confess, "I have you on my nerves!") Paul's sincere love for his friends was something that could not be disguised or hidden.

Christian love is "the tie that binds." Love is the evidence of salvation: "We know that we have passed from death unto life, because we love the brethren" (1 John 3:14). It is the "spiritual lubrication" that keeps the machinery of life running smoothly. Have you noticed how often Paul used the phrase "you all" as he wrote? There are at least nine instances in this letter. He did not want to leave anyone out! (Some translations read, "You have me in your heart" in Phil. 1:7, but the basic truth is the same.)

How did Paul evidence his love for them? For one thing, he was suffering on their behalf. His bonds were proof of his love. He was "the prisoner of Jesus Christ for you Gentiles" (Eph. 3:1). Because of Paul's trial, Christianity was going to get a fair hearing before the officials of Rome. Since Philippi was a Roman colony, the decision would affect the believers there. Paul's love was not something he merely talked about; it was something he practiced. He considered his difficult circumstances an opportunity for defending and confirming the gospel, and this would help his brethren everywhere.

But how can Christians learn to practice this kind of love? "I get along better with my unsaved neighbors than I do my saved relatives!" a man confided to his pastor. "Maybe it takes a diamond to cut a diamond, but I've just about had it!" Christian love is not something we work up; it is something that God does in us and through us. Paul longed for his friends "in the bowels [love] of Jesus Christ" (Phil. 1:8). It was not Paul's love channeled through Christ; it was Christ's love channeled through Paul. "God has poured out his love into our hearts by the Holy Spirit, whom he has given us" (Rom. 5:5 NIV). When we permit God to perform His "good work" in us, then we grow in our love for one another.

How can we tell that we are truly bound in love to other Christians? For one thing, we are concerned about them. The believers at Philippi were concerned about Paul and sent Epaphroditus to minister to him. Paul was also greatly concerned about his friends at Philippi, especially when Epaphroditus became ill and could not return right away (Phil. 2:25–28). "My little children, let us not love in word, neither in tongue; but in deed and in truth" (1 John 3:18).

Another evidence of Christian love is a willingness to forgive one another. "And above all things have fervent charity [love] among yourselves: for charity [love] shall cover the multitude of sins" (1 Peter 4:8).

"Tell us some of the blunders your wife has made," a radio quizmaster asked a contestant.

"I can't remember any," the man replied.

"Oh, surely you can remember something!" the announcer said.

"No, I really can't," the contestant said. "I love my wife very much, and I just don't remember things like that." First Corinthians 13:5 states that love "keeps no record of wrongs" (NIV).

Christians who practice love always experience joy; both come as a result of the presence of the same Holy Spirit. "The fruit of the Spirit is love, joy" (Gal. 5:22).

I Have You in My Prayers (1:9–11)

Paul found joy in his memories of the friends at Philippi and in his growing love for them. He also found joy in remembering them before the throne of grace in prayer. The high priest in the Old Testament wore a special garment, the ephod, over his heart. On it were twelve stones with the names of the twelve tribes of Israel engraved on them, a jewel for each tribe (Ex. 28:15–29). He carried the people over his heart in love, and so did Paul. Perhaps the deepest Christian fellowship and joy we can experience in this life is at the throne of grace, praying with and for one another.

This is a prayer for maturity, and Paul began with *love*. After all, if our Christian love is what it ought to be, everything else should follow. He prayed that they might experience *abounding* love and *discerning* love. Christian love is not blind! The heart and mind work together so that we have discerning love and loving discernment. Paul wanted his friends to grow in discernment, in being able to "distinguish the things that differ."

The ability to distinguish is a mark of maturity. When a baby learns to speak, he or she may call every four-legged animal a "bowwow." But then the child discovers that there are cats, white mice, cows, and other four-legged creatures. To a little child, one automobile is just like another, but not to a car-crazy teenager! He can spot the differences between models faster than his parents can even name the cars! One of the sure marks of maturity is discerning love.

Paul also prayed that they might have mature Christian *character*, "sincere and without offence." The Greek word translated "sincere" may have several meanings. Some translate it "tested by sunlight." The sincere Christian is not afraid to "stand in the light."

Sincere may also mean "to whirl in a sieve," suggesting the idea of a winnowing process that removes chaff. In both cases the truth is the same: Paul prayed that his friends would have the kind of character that can pass the test. (Our English word *sincere* comes from a Latin word that means "unadulterated, pure, unmixed.")

Paul prayed for them to have mature Christian love and character, "without offense till the day of Christ" (Phil. 1:10). This means that our lives do not cause others to stumble, and that they are ready for the judgment seat of Christ when He returns (see 2 Cor. 5:10; 1 John 2:28). Here are two good tests for us to follow as we exercise spiritual discernment: (1) Will it make others stumble? (2) Will it make me ashamed if Jesus should return?

Paul also prayed that they might have mature Christian *service*. He wanted them filled and fruitful (Phil. 1:11). He was not interested simply in church activities, but in the kind of spiritual fruit that is produced when we are in fellowship with Christ. "Abide in me, and I in you. As the branch cannot bear fruit of itself, except it abide in the vine; no more can ye, except ye abide in me" (John 15:4). Too many Christians try to produce results in their own efforts instead of abiding in Christ and allowing His life to produce the fruit.

What is the "fruit" God wants to see from our lives? Certainly He wants the "fruit of the Spirit" (Gal. 5:22–23), Christian character that glorifies God. Paul compared winning lost souls to Christ to bearing fruit (Rom. 1:13), and he also names "holiness" as a spiritual fruit (Rom. 6:22). He exhorted us to be "fruitful in every good work" (Col. 1:10), and the writer to the Hebrews reminded us that our praise is the "fruit of our lips" (Heb. 13:15).

The fruit tree does not make a great deal of noise when it produces its crop; it merely allows the life within to work in a natural way, and fruit is the result. "He that abideth in me, and I in him, the same bringeth forth much fruit: for without me ye can do nothing" (John 15:5).

The difference between spiritual fruit and human religious activity is that the fruit brings glory to Jesus Christ. Whenever we do anything in our own strength, we have a tendency to boast about it. True spiritual fruit is so beautiful and wonderful that no human can claim credit for it; the glory must go to God alone.

This, then, is true Christian fellowship—a having-in-common that is much deeper than mere friendship. "I have you in my mind … I have you in my heart … I have you in my prayers." This is the kind of fellowship that produces joy, *and it is the single mind that produces this kind of fellowship.*

Jerry had to go to New York City for special surgery, and he hated to go. "Why can't we have it done at home?" he asked his doctor. "I don't know a soul in that big, unfriendly city!" But when he and his wife arrived at the hospital, there was a pastor to meet them and invite them to stay at his home until they got settled. The operation was serious, and the wait in the hospital was long and difficult, but the fellowship of the pastor and his wife brought a new joy to Jerry and his wife. They learned that circumstances need not rob us of joy if we will but permit these circumstances to strengthen the fellowship of the gospel.

QUESTIONS FOR PERSONAL REFLECTION
OR GROUP DISCUSSION

1. What is redemption and why is it essential to the Christian life? How does this affect your everyday living?

2. What is sanctification and why is it essential to the Christian life? Where do you see this occurring in your own life?

3. What is service and why is it essential to the Christian life? How can you improve this area of your own life?

4. What is the "spiritual lubrication that keeps the machinery of life running smoothly"? Explain.

5. A popular song says "all you need is love." Is that true? Why or why not?

6. How can we tell when we are truly "bound in love" to other Christians?

7. Why is forgiveness one of the most difficult but significant evidences of genuine love?

8. How can praying for other Christians (especially those with whom we have some friction) improve our fellowship with them?

9. What is the difference between spiritual fruit and religious activity?

10. What is true Christian fellowship?

Chapter Three

PIONEERS WANTED

(Philippians 1:12–26)

More than anything else, Paul's desire as a missionary was to preach the gospel in Rome. The hub of the great empire, Rome was the key city of its day. If Paul could conquer it for Christ, it would mean reaching millions with the message of salvation. It was critically important on Paul's agenda, for he said, "After I have been there [Jerusalem], I must also see Rome" (Acts 19:21). From Corinth he wrote, "So, as much as in me is, I am ready [eager] to preach the gospel to you that are at Rome also" (Rom. 1:15).

Paul wanted to go to Rome as a preacher, but instead he went as *a prisoner.* He could have written a long letter about that experience alone. Instead, he summed it all up as "the things which happened unto me" (Phil. 1:12). The record of these things is given in Acts 21:17—28:31, and it begins with Paul's illegal arrest in the temple in Jerusalem. The Jews thought he had desecrated their temple by bringing in Gentiles, and the Romans thought he was an Egyptian renegade who was on their most-wanted list. Paul became the focal point of both political and religious plotting and remained a prisoner in Caesarea for two years. When he finally appealed to Caesar (which was the privilege of every Roman citizen), he was sent to Rome. En route, the ship was wrecked. The account of that storm and Paul's courage and faith is one of the most dramatic in the Bible (Acts 27). After three months of waiting on the Island of Malta, Paul finally embarked for Rome and the trial he had requested before Caesar.

To many, all of this would have looked like failure, but not to this man with a "single mind," concerned with sharing Christ and the gospel. Paul did not find his joy in ideal circumstances; he found his joy in winning others to Christ. And if his circumstances promoted the furtherance of the gospel, that was all that mattered. The word *furtherance* means "pioneer advance." It is a Greek military term referring to the army engineers who go before the troops to open the way into new territory. Instead of finding himself confined as a prisoner, Paul discovered that his circumstances really opened up new areas of ministry.

Everyone has heard of Charles Haddon Spurgeon, the famous British preacher, but few know the story of his wife, Susannah. Early in their married life, Mrs. Spurgeon became an invalid. It looked as though her only ministry would be encouraging her husband and praying for his work. But God gave her a burden to share her husband's books with pastors who were unable to purchase them. This burden soon led to the founding of the Book Fund. As a work of faith, the Book Fund provided thousands of pastors with tools for their work. All this was supervised by Mrs. Spurgeon from her home. It was a pioneer ministry.

God still wants His children to take the gospel into new areas. He wants us to be pioneers, and sometimes He arranges circumstances so that we can be nothing else but pioneers. In fact, that is how the gospel originally came to Philippi. Paul had tried to enter other territory, but God had repeatedly shut the door (Acts 16:6–10). Paul wanted to take the message eastward into Asia, but God directed him to take it westward into Europe. What a difference it would have made in the history of mankind if Paul had been permitted to follow his own plan.

God sometimes uses strange tools to help us pioneer the gospel. In Paul's case, there were three tools that helped him take the gospel even into the elite Praetorian Guard, Caesar's special troops: his *chains* (Phil. 1:12–14), his *critics* (Phil. 1:15–19), and his *crisis* (Phil. 1:20–26).

1. Paul's Chains (1:12–14)

The same God who used Moses' rod, Gideon's pitchers, and David's sling used Paul's chains. Little did the Romans realize that the chains they affixed to his wrists would *release* Paul instead of *bind* him. Even as he wrote during a later imprisonment, "I suffer trouble, as an evildoer, even unto bonds; but the word of God is not bound" (2 Tim. 2:9). He did not complain about his chains; instead, he consecrated them to God and asked God to use them for the pioneer advance of the gospel. And God answered his prayers.

To begin with, these chains gave Paul *contact with the lost.* He was chained to a Roman soldier twenty-four hours a day. The shifts changed every six hours, which meant Paul could witness to at least four men each day. Imagine yourself as one of those soldiers, chained to a man who prayed "without ceasing," who was constantly interviewing people about their spiritual condition, and who was repeatedly writing letters to Christians and churches throughout the empire. It was not long before some of these soldiers put their faith in Christ. Paul was able to get the gospel into the elite Praetorian Guard, something he could not have done had he been a free man.

But the chains gave Paul contact with another group of people: the officials in Caesar's court. He was in Rome as an official prisoner, and his case was an important one. The Roman government was going to determine the official status of this new "Christian" sect. Was it merely another sect of the Jews? Or was it something new and possibly dangerous? Imagine how pleased Paul must have been knowing that the court officials were forced to study the doctrines of the Christian faith.

Sometimes God has to put "chains" on His people to get them to accomplish a "pioneer advance" that could never happen any other way. Young mothers may feel chained to the home as they care for their children, but God can use those chains to reach people with the message of salvation. Susannah Wesley was the mother of nineteen children, before the days of labor-saving devices and disposable diapers. Out of that large family came John and Charles Wesley, whose combined ministries shook the British Isles. At six weeks of age, Fanny Crosby was blinded, but even as a youngster she determined not to be confined by the chains of darkness. In time, she became a mighty force for God through her hymns and gospel songs.

The secret is this: When you have the single mind, you look on your circumstances as God-given opportunities for the furtherance of the gospel, and you rejoice at *what God is going to do* instead of complaining about *what God did not do.*

Paul's chains not only gave contact with the lost, but they also gave *courage to the saved.* Many of the believers in Rome took fresh courage when they saw Paul's faith and determination (Phil. 1:14). They were "much more bold to speak the word without fear." That word *speak* does not mean "preach." Rather, it means "everyday conversation." No doubt many of the Romans were discussing Paul's case, because such legal matters were of primary concern to this nation of lawmakers. And the Christians in Rome who were sympathetic to Paul took advantage of this conversation to say a good word for Jesus Christ. Discouragement has a way of spreading, but so does encouragement. Because of Paul's joyful attitude, the believers in Rome took fresh courage and witnessed boldly for Christ.

While recovering in the hospital from a serious auto accident, I received a letter from a total stranger who seemed to know just what to say to make my day brighter. In fact, I received several letters from him, and each one was better than the one before. When I was able to get around, I met him personally. I was amazed to discover that he was blind, a diabetic, handicapped because of a leg amputation (and since then the other leg has been removed), and that he lived with and cared for his elderly mother! If a man ever wore chains, this man did. But if a man ever was free to pioneer the gospel, this man was. He was able to share Christ in high school assemblies, before service clubs, at the Y, and before professional people in meetings that would have been closed to an ordained minister. My friend had the single mind; he lived for Christ and the gospel. Consequently, he shared the joy of furthering the gospel.

Our chains may not be as dramatic or difficult, but there is no reason why God cannot use them in the same way.

2. PAUL'S CRITICS (1:15–19)

It is hard to believe that anyone would oppose Paul, but there were believers in Rome doing just that. The churches there were divided. Some preached Christ sincerely, wanting to see people saved. Some preached Christ insincerely, wanting to make the situation more difficult for Paul. The latter group was using the gospel to further their own selfish purposes. Perhaps they belonged to the legalistic wing of the church that opposed Paul's ministry to the Gentiles and his emphasis on the grace of God as opposed to obedience to the Jewish law. Envy and strife go together, just as love and unity go together.

Paul used an interesting word in Philippians 1:16—*contention*. It means "to canvass for office, to get people to support you." Paul's aim was to glorify Christ and get people to follow Him; his critics' aim was to promote themselves and win a following of their own. Instead of asking, "Have you trusted Christ?" they asked, "Whose side are you on—ours or Paul's?" Unfortunately, this kind of religious politics is still seen today. And the people who practice it need to realize that they are only hurting themselves.

When you have the single mind, you look on your critics as another opportunity for the furtherance of the gospel. Like a faithful soldier, Paul was "set [appointed] for the defence of the gospel" (Phil. 1:17). He was able to rejoice, not in the selfishness of his critics, but in the fact that *Christ was being preached!* There was no envy in Paul's heart. It mattered not that some were for him and some were against him. All that mattered was the preaching of the gospel of Jesus Christ!

It is a matter of historic record that the two great English evangelists, John Wesley and George Whitefield, disagreed on doctrinal matters. Both of them were very successful, preaching to thousands of people and seeing multitudes come to Christ. It is reported that somebody asked Wesley if he expected to see Whitefield in heaven, and the evangelist replied, "No, I do not."

"Then you do not think Whitefield is a converted man?"

"Of course he is a converted man!" Wesley said. "But I do not expect to see him in heaven—because he will be so close to the throne of God and I so far away that I will not be able to see him." Though he differed with his brother in some matters, Wesley did not have any envy in his heart, nor did he seek to oppose Whitefield's ministry.

Criticism is usually very hard to take, particularly when we are in difficult circumstances, as Paul was. How was the apostle able to rejoice even in the face of such diverse criticism? He possessed the single mind. Philippians 1:19 indicates that Paul expected his case to turn out victoriously ("to my salvation") because of the prayers of his friends and the supply of the Holy Spirit of God. The word *supply* gives us our English word *chorus.* Whenever a Greek city was going to put on a special festival, somebody had to pay for the singers and dancers. The donation called for had to be a lavish one, and so this word came to mean "to provide generously and lavishly." Paul was not depending on his own dwindling resources; he was depending on the generous resources of God, ministered by the Holy Spirit.

Paul shared in the pioneer advance of the gospel in Rome through his chains and his critics, but he had a third tool that he used.

3. PAUL'S CRISIS (1:20–26)

Because of Paul's chains, Christ was *known* (Phil. 1:13), and because of Paul's critics, Christ was *preached* (Phil. 1:18). But because of Paul's crisis, Christ was *magnified!* (Phil. 1:20). It was possible that Paul would be found a traitor to Rome and then executed. His preliminary trial had apparently gone in his favor. The final verdict, however, was yet to come. But Paul's body was not his own, and his only desire (because he had the single mind) was to magnify Christ in his body.

Does Christ need to be magnified? After all, how can a mere human being ever magnify the Son of God? Well, the stars are much bigger than the telescope, and yet the telescope magnifies them and brings them closer. The believer's body is to be a telescope that brings Jesus Christ close to people. To the average person, Christ is a misty figure in history who lived centuries ago. But as the unsaved watch the believer go through a crisis, they can see Jesus magnified and brought so much closer. To the Christian with the single mind, Christ is with us here and now.

The telescope brings distant things closer, and the microscope makes tiny things look big. To the unbeliever, Jesus is not very big. Other people and other things are far more important. But as the unbeliever watches the Christian go through a crisis experience, he ought to be able to see how big Jesus Christ really is. The believer's body is a lens that makes a little Christ look very big, and a distant Christ come very close.

Paul was not afraid of life or death. Either way, he wanted to magnify Christ in his body. No wonder he had joy!

Paul confessed that he was facing a difficult decision. To remain alive was necessary for the believers' benefit in Philippi, but to depart and be with Christ was far better. Paul decided that Christ would have him remain, not only for the "furtherance of the gospel" (Phil. 1:12) but also for the "furtherance and joy of [their] faith" (Phil. 1:25). He wanted them to make some "pioneer advance" into new areas of spiritual growth. (By the way, Paul admonished Timothy, the young pastor, to be sure to pioneer new spiritual territory in his own life and ministry. See 1 Tim. 4:15, where "profiting" is our phrase "pioneer advance.")

What a man Paul was! He was willing to postpone going to heaven in order to help Christians grow, and he was willing to go to hell in order to win the lost to Christ (Rom. 9:1–3).

Of course, death had no terrors for Paul. It simply meant "departing." This word was used by soldiers; it meant "to take down your tent and move on." What a picture of Christian death! The "tent" we live in is taken down at death, and the spirit goes home to be with Christ in heaven. (Read 2 Cor. 5:1–8.) Sailors also used this word; it meant "to loosen a ship and set sail." Lord Tennyson used this figure of death in his famous poem "Crossing the Bar."

But *departure* was also a political term; it described the setting free of a prisoner. God's people are in bondage because of the limitations of the body and the temptations of the flesh, but death will free them. Or they will be freed at the return of Christ (Rom. 8:18–23) if that should come first. Finally, *departure* was a word used by farmers; it meant "to unyoke the oxen." Paul had taken Christ's yoke, which is an easy yoke to bear (Matt. 11:28–30), but how many burdens he carried in his ministry! (If you need your memory refreshed, read 2 Cor. 11:22—12:10.) To depart to be with Christ would mean laying aside the burdens, his earthly work completed.

No matter how you look at it, nothing can steal a man's joy if he possesses the single mind. "For to me to live is Christ, and to die is gain" (Phil. 1:21). Maltbie Babcock, who wrote "This Is My Father's World," said, "Life is what we are alive to." When my wife and I go shopping, I dread going to the fabric department, but I often have to go because my wife enjoys looking at fabrics. If on the way to the fabric section I spot the book department, I suddenly come alive. The thing that excites us and motivates us is the thing that really is "life" to us. In Paul's case, Christ was his life. Christ excited him and made his life worth living.

Philippians 1:21 becomes a valuable test of our lives. "For to me to live is _____ and to die is _____." Fill in the blanks yourself.

"For to me to live is *money* and to die is *to leave it all behind.*"

"For to me to live is *fame* and to die is *to be forgotten.*"

"For to me to live is *power* and to die is *to lose it all.*"

No, we must echo Paul's convictions if we are going to have joy in spite of circumstances, and if we are going to share in the furtherance of the gospel. "For to me to live is *Christ*, and to die is *gain*."

QUESTIONS FOR PERSONAL REFLECTION
OR GROUP DISCUSSION

1. How did Paul's circumstances open up new areas of ministry for him rather than confine him?

2. How did God use the chains on Paul's wrists to advance the gospel?

3. How did Paul's circumstances encourage many believers in Rome?

4. What kinds of "chains" in your life has God used?

5. Why was Paul able to rejoice in the face of criticism?

6. How can Christ be magnified through a crisis in your life?

7. How does your answer to the previous question change your attitude about the bad things that happen to you?

8. There's an old Christian chorus that says, "Do you know, oh Christian, you're a sermon in shoes?" What does that mean?

9. How are Christians in bondage while we live on earth? How will death free us?

10. How can each of us be a pioneer for Christ?

Chapter Four

BATTLE STATIONS!

(Philippians 1:27–30)

The Christian life is not a playground; it is a battleground. We are *sons* in the family, enjoying the *fellowship* of the gospel (Phil. 1:1–11); we are *servants* sharing in the *furtherance* of the gospel (Phil. 1:12–26); but we are also *soldiers* defending the *faith* of the gospel. And the believer with the single mind can have the joy of the Holy Spirit even in the midst of battle.

"The faith of the gospel" is that body of divine truth given to the church. Jude called it "the faith which was once delivered unto the saints" (Jude 3). Paul warned in 1 Timothy 4:1 that "in the latter times some shall depart from the faith." God committed this spiritual treasure to Paul (1 Tim. 1:11), and he in turn committed it to others, like Timothy (1 Tim. 6:20), whose responsibility was to commit this deposit to still others (2 Tim. 2:2). This is why the church must engage in a teaching ministry, so that each new generation of believers will know, appreciate, and use the great heritage of the faith.

But there is an enemy who is out to steal the treasure from God's people. Paul had met the enemy in Philippi, and he was now facing him in Rome. If Satan can only rob believers of their Christian faith, the doctrines that are distinctively theirs, then he can cripple and defeat the ministry of the gospel. It is sad to hear people say, "I don't care what you believe, just so long as you live right." What we believe determines how we behave, and wrong belief ultimately means a wrong life. Each local church is but one generation short of potential extinction. No wonder Satan attacks our young people in particular, seeking to get them away from the faith.

How can a group of Christians fight this enemy? "For the weapons of our warfare are not of the flesh" (2 Cor. 10:4 NASB). Peter took up a sword in the garden, and Jesus rebuked him (John 18:10–11). We use spiritual weapons—the Word of God and prayer (Eph. 6:11–18; Heb. 4:12), and we must depend on the Holy Spirit to give us the power that we need. But an army must fight *together*, and this is why Paul sent these admonitions to his friends at Philippi. He was explaining in this paragraph that there are three essentials for victory in the battle to protect the faith.

1. CONSISTENCY (1:27A)

The old English word *conversation*, of course, means *walk* and not *talk*. "Only conduct yourselves in a manner worthy of the gospel of Christ" (NASB). The most important weapon against the enemy is not a stirring sermon or a powerful book; it is the consistent life of believers.

The verb Paul used is related to our word *politics*. He was saying, "Behave the way citizens are supposed to behave." My wife and I were visiting in London and one day decided to go to the zoo. We boarded the bus and sat back to enjoy the ride, but it was impossible to enjoy it because of the loud, coarse conversation of the passengers at the front of the bus. Unfortunately, they were Americans, and we could see the British around us raising their eyebrows and shaking their heads, as though to say, "Oh, yes, they're from America!" We were embarrassed because we knew that these people did not really represent the best of American citizens.

Paul was suggesting that we Christians are the citizens of heaven, and while we are on earth we ought to behave like heaven's citizens. He brought this concept up again in Philippians 3:20. It would be a very meaningful expression to the people in Philippi because Philippi was a Roman colony, and its citizens were actually Roman citizens, protected by Roman law. The church of Jesus Christ is a colony of heaven on earth. And we ought to behave like the citizens of heaven.

"Am I conducting myself in a manner worthy of the gospel?" is a good question for us to ask ourselves regularly. We should "walk … worthy of the calling" that we have in Christ (Eph. 4:1 NASB), which means walking "worthy of the Lord unto all pleasing" (Col. 1:10). We do not behave in order to go to heaven, as though we could be saved by our good works; but we behave because our names are already written in heaven, and our citizenship is in heaven.

It is worth remembering that the world around us knows only the gospel that it sees in our lives.

> You are writing a gospel,
> A chapter each day,
> By the deeds that you do
> And the words that you say.
> Men read what you write,
> Whether faithful or true:
> Just what is the gospel
> According to you?
>
> —SOURCE UNKNOWN

"The gospel" is the good news that Christ died for our sins, was buried, and rose again (1 Cor. 15:1–8). There is only one "good news" of salvation; any other gospel is false (Gal. 1:6–10). The message of the gospel is the good news that sinners can become the children of God through faith in Jesus Christ, God's Son (John 3:16). To add anything to the gospel is to deprive it of its power. We are not saved from our sins by faith in Christ *plus* something else; we are saved by faith in Christ *alone*.

"We have some neighbors who believe a false gospel," a church member told his pastor. "Do you have some literature I can give them?"

The pastor opened his Bible to 2 Corinthians 3:2: "You are our letter, written in our hearts, known and read by all men" (NASB). He said, "The best literature in the world is no substitute for your own life. Let them see Christ in your behavior, and this will open up opportunities to share Christ's gospel with them."

The greatest weapon against the Devil is a godly life. And a local church that practices the truth, that "behaves what it believes," is going to defeat the enemy. This is the first essential for victory in this battle.

2. Cooperation (1:27b)

Paul now changed the illustration from politics to athletics. The word translated "striving together" gives us our English word *athletics*. Paul pictured the church as a team, and he reminded them that it is teamwork that wins victories.

Keep in mind that there was division in the church at Philippi. For one thing, two women were not getting along with each other (Phil. 4:2). Apparently the members of the fellowship were taking sides, as is often the case, and the resulting division was hindering the work of the church. The enemy is always happy to see internal divisions in a local ministry. "Divide and conquer!" is his motto, and too often he has his way. It is only as believers stand together that they can overcome the wicked one.

Throughout this letter, Paul used an interesting device to emphasize the importance of unity. In the Greek language, the prefix *sun-* means "with, together," and when used with different words, strengthens the idea of unity. (It is somewhat like our prefix *co-*.) At least sixteen times, Paul used this prefix in Philippians, and his readers could not have missed the message. In Philippians 1:27, the Greek word is *sunathleo*—"striving together as athletes."

Jerry was disgusted, and he decided to tell the coach how he felt. "There's no sense coming out for practice anymore," he complained. "Mike is the team—you don't need the rest of us."

Coach Gardner knew the trouble. "Look, Jerry, just because Mike gets many of the chances to shoot doesn't mean the rest of you guys aren't needed. Somebody has to set things up at the basket, and that's where you come in."

Sometimes a team has a "glory hound" who has to be in the spotlight and get all the praise. Usually he makes it difficult for the rest of the team. They aren't working equally together but are working to make one person look good. It is this attitude that makes for defeat. Unfortunately, we have some glory hounds in the church. John had to deal with a man named Diotrephes because the man loved "to have the preeminence" (3 John 9). Even the apostles James and John asked to have special thrones (Matt. 20:20–28). The important word is *together:* standing firmly together in one spirit, striving together against the enemy, and doing it with one mind and heart.

It would not be difficult to expand this idea of the local church as a team of athletes. Each person has his assigned place and job, and if each one is doing his job, it helps all the others. Not everybody can be captain or quarterback. The team has to follow the rules, and the Word of God is our rule book. There is one goal—to honor Christ and do His will. If we all work together, we can reach the goal, win the prize, and glorify the Lord. But the minute any one of us starts disobeying the rules, breaking training (the Christian life does demand discipline), or looking for glory, the teamwork disappears and division and competition take over.

In other words, Paul was reminding us again of the need for *the single mind*. There is joy in our lives, even as we battle the enemy, if we live for Christ and the gospel and practice Christian teamwork. To be sure, there are some people with whom we cannot cooperate (2 Cor. 6:14–18; Eph. 5:11), but there are many with whom we *can*—and should!

We are citizens of heaven and therefore should walk consistently. We are members of the same "team" and should work cooperatively. But there is a third essential for success as we face the enemy, and that is *confidence*.

3. CONFIDENCE (1:28–30)

"Don't be alarmed by your opponents!" The word Paul used pictures a horse shying away from battle. To be sure, nobody blindly runs into a fight, but then, no true believer should deliberately avoid facing the enemy. In these verses, Paul gave us several encouragements that give us confidence in the battle.

First, *these battles prove that we are saved* (Phil. 1:29). We not only believe in Christ but also suffer for Christ. Paul called this "the fellowship of his sufferings" (Phil. 3:10). For some reason, many new believers have the idea that trusting Christ means the end of their battles. In reality, it means the beginning of *new* battles. "In the world ye shall have tribulation" (John 16:33). "Yea, and all that will live godly in Christ Jesus shall suffer persecution" (2 Tim. 3:12).

But the presence of conflict is *a privilege;* we suffer "for his sake." In fact, Paul told us that this conflict is "granted" to us—it is a gift! If we were suffering for ourselves, it would be no privilege, but because we are suffering for and with Christ, it is a high and holy honor. After all, He suffered for us, and a willingness to suffer for Him is the very least we can do to show our love and gratitude.

A third encouragement is this: *Others are experiencing the same conflict* (Phil. 1:30). Satan wants us to think we are alone in the battle, that our difficulties are unique, but such is not the case. Paul reminded the Philippians that he was going through the same difficulties they were experiencing hundreds of miles from Rome! A change in geography is usually no solution to spiritual problems, because human nature is the same wherever you go, and the enemy is everywhere. Knowing that my fellow believers are also sharing in the battle is an encouragement for me to keep going and to pray for them as I pray for myself.

Actually, going through spiritual conflict is one way we have *to grow in Christ.* God gives us the strength we need to stand firm against the enemy, and this confidence is proof to him that he will lose and we are on the winning side (Phil. 1:28). The Philippians had seen Paul go through conflict when he was with them (read Acts 16:19ff.), and they had witnessed his firmness in the Lord. The word *conflict* gives us our word *agony (agonia),* and is the same word that is used for Christ's struggle in the garden (Luke 22:44). As we face the enemy and depend on the Lord, He gives us all that we need for the battle. When the enemy sees our God-given confidence, it makes him fear.

So the single mind enables us to have joy in the midst of battle because it produces in us *consistency*, *cooperation*, and *confidence*. We experience the joy of "spiritual teamwork" as we strive together for the faith of the gospel.

QUESTIONS FOR PERSONAL REFLECTION
OR GROUP DISCUSSION

1. What is "the faith of the gospel" that we are defending?

2. Why is it so important for a Christian to know what he or she believes?

3. What are some of the spiritual weapons we can use in our battle against Satan?

4. What is our most important weapon against the enemy? How can you make better use of this weapon in your own life?

5. Why is consistency in the Christian life so important?

6. What does it mean to "walk worthy of the calling" that we have in Christ (Eph. 4:1 NIV)?

7. Why is Satan happy when he sees conflict and divisions in a church?

8. How do the battles in our lives prove that we're saved?

9. Why does Satan want Christians to think we're alone in our battles? Who do you turn to during these times?

10. How does going through spiritual conflict help us grow in Christ?

Chapter Five

THE GREAT EXAMPLE

(Philippians 2:1–11)

People can rob us of our joy. Paul was facing his problems with people at Rome (Phil. 1:15–18) as well as with people in Philippi, and it was the latter who concerned him the most. When Epaphroditus brought a generous gift from the church in Philippi, and good news of the church's concern for Paul, he also brought the bad news of a possible division in the church family. Apparently there was a double threat to the unity of the church: false teachers coming in from without (Phil. 3:1–3) and disagreeing members within (Phil. 4:1–3). What Euodia ("fragrance") and Syntyche ("fortunate") were debating about, Paul did not state. Perhaps they both wanted to be president of the missionary guild or the choir!

Paul knew what some church workers today do not know: There is a difference between *unity* and *uniformity*. True spiritual unity comes from within; it is a matter of the heart. Uniformity is the result of pressure from without. This is why Paul opened this section appealing to the highest possible spiritual motives (Phil. 2:1–4). Since the believers at Philippi were "in Christ," this ought to have encouraged them to work toward unity and love, not division and rivalry. In a gracious way, Paul was saying to the church, "Your disagreements reveal that there is a spiritual problem in your fellowship. It isn't going to be solved by rules or threats; it's going to be solved when your hearts are right with Christ and with each other." Paul wanted them to see that the basic cause was *selfishness,* and the cause of selfishness is *pride.* There can be no joy in the life of the Christian who puts himself above others.

The secret of joy in spite of circumstances is *the single mind.* The secret of joy in spite of people is *the submissive mind.* The key verse is "Let nothing be done through strife or vainglory; but in lowliness of mind let each esteem other better [more important] than themselves" (Phil. 2:3). In Philippians 1, it is "Christ first" and in Philippians 2 it is "others next." Paul the soul winner in Philippians 1 becomes Paul the servant in Philippians 2.

It is important that we understand what the Bible means by "humility." The humble person is not one who thinks meanly of himself; he simply does not think of himself at all! (I think Andrew Murray said that.) Humility is that grace that, when you know you have it, you have lost it. The truly humble person knows himself and accepts himself (Rom. 12:3). He yields himself to Christ to be a servant, to use what he is and has for the glory of God and the good of others. "Others" is the key idea in this chapter (Phil. 2:3–4); the believer's eyes are turned away from himself and focused on the needs of others.

The "submissive mind" does not mean that the believer is at the beck and call of everybody else or that he is a "religious doormat" for everybody to use. Some people try to purchase friends and maintain church unity by giving in to everybody else's whims and wishes. This is not what Paul is suggesting at all. The Scripture puts it perfectly: "ourselves your servants for Jesus' sake" (2 Cor. 4:5). If we have the single mind of Philippians 1, then we will have no problem with the submissive mind of Philippians 2.

Paul gave us four examples of the submissive mind: Jesus Christ

(Phil. 2:1–11), Paul himself (Phil. 2:12–18), Timothy (Phil. 2:19–24), and Epaphroditus (Phil. 2:25–30). Of course, the great example is Jesus, and Paul began with Him. Jesus Christ illustrates the four characteristics of the person with the submissive mind.

1. He Thinks of Others, Not Himself (2:5–6)

The "mind" of Christ means the "attitude" Christ exhibited. "Your attitude should be the same as that of Christ Jesus" (Phil. 2:5 NIV). After all, outlook determines outcome. If the outlook is selfish, the actions will be divisive and destructive. James said the same thing (see James 4:1–10).

These verses in Philippians take us to eternity past. "Form of God" has nothing to do with shape or size. God is Spirit (John 4:24), and as such is not to be thought of in human terms. When the Bible refers to "the eyes of the Lord" or "the hand of the Lord," it is not claiming that God has a human shape. Rather, it is using human terms to describe divine attributes (the characteristics of God) and activities. The word *form* means "the outward expression of the inward nature." This means that in eternity past, *Jesus Christ was God.* In fact, Paul stated that Jesus was "equal with God." Other verses such as John 1:1–4; Colossians 1:15; and Hebrews 1:1–3 also state that Jesus Christ is God.

Certainly as God, Jesus Christ did not need anything. He had all the glory and praise of heaven. With the Father and the Spirit, He reigned over the universe. But Philippians 2:6 states an amazing fact: He did not consider His equality with God as something selfishly to be held on to. Jesus did not think of Himself; He thought of others. His outlook (or attitude) was that of unselfish concern for others. This is "the mind of Christ," an attitude that says, "I cannot keep my privileges for myself, I must use them for others, and to do this, I will gladly lay them aside and pay whatever price is necessary."

A reporter was interviewing a successful job counselor who had placed hundreds of workers in their vocations quite happily. When asked the secret of his success, the man replied, "If you want to find out what a worker is really like, don't give him responsibilities—give him *privileges*. Most people can handle responsibilities if you pay them enough, but it takes a real leader to handle privileges. A leader will use his privileges to help others and build the organization; a lesser man will use privileges to promote himself." Jesus used His heavenly privileges for the sake of others—for *our* sake.

It would be worthwhile to contrast Christ's attitude with that of Lucifer (Isa. 14:12–15) and Adam (Gen. 3:1–7). Many Bible students believe that the fall of Lucifer is a description of the fall of Satan. He once was the highest of the angelic beings, close to the throne of God (Ezek. 28:11–19), but he desired to be *on* the throne of God! Lucifer said, "I will!" but Jesus said, *"Thy* will." Lucifer was not satisfied to be a creature; he wanted to be the Creator. Jesus was the Creator, yet He willingly became man. Christ's humility is a rebuke to Satan's pride.

Lucifer was not satisfied to be a rebel himself; he invaded Eden and tempted man to be a rebel. Adam had all that he needed; he was actually the "king" of God's creation ("let them have dominion," Gen. 1:26). But Satan said, "You will be like God!" Man deliberately grasped after something that was beyond his reach, and as a result plunged the whole human race into sin and death. Adam and Eve thought only of themselves; Jesus Christ thought of others.

We expect unsaved people to be selfish and grasping, but we do not expect this of Christians, who have experienced the love of Christ and the fellowship of the Spirit (Phil. 2:1–2). More than twenty times in the New Testament, God instructs us how to live with "one another." We are to prefer one another (Rom. 12:10), edify one another (1 Thess. 5:11), and bear each other's burdens (Gal. 6:2). We should not judge one another (Rom. 14:13) but rather admonish one another (Rom. 15:14). *Others* is the key word in the vocabulary of the Christian who exercises the submissive mind.

2. He Serves (2:7)

Thinking of "others" in an abstract sense only is insufficient; we must get down to the nitty-gritty of true service. A famous philosopher wrote glowing words about educating children but abandoned his own. It was easy for him to love children in the abstract, but when it came down to practice, that was something else. Jesus thought of others *and became a servant.* Paul traced the steps in the humiliation of Christ: (1) He emptied Himself, laying aside the independent use of His own attributes as God; (2) He permanently became a human, in a sinless physical body; (3) He used that body to be a servant; (4) He took that body to the cross and willingly died.

What grace! From heaven to earth, from glory to shame, from Master to servant, from life to death, "even the death of the cross" (v. 8). In the Old Testament age, Christ had visited earth on occasion for some special ministry (Gen. 18 is a case in point), but these visits were temporary. When Christ was born at Bethlehem, He entered into a *permanent* union with humanity from which there could be no escape. He willingly humbled Himself that He might lift us up. Note that Paul used the word *form* again in Philippians 2:7, "the outward expression of the inward nature." Jesus did not pretend to be a servant; He was not an actor playing a role. *He actually was a servant.* This was the true expression of His innermost nature. He was the God-Man, Deity and humanity united in one, and He came as a servant.

Have you noticed as you read the four gospels that it is Jesus who serves others, not others who serve Jesus? He is at the beck and call of all kinds of people—fishermen, harlots, tax collectors, the sick, the sorrowing. "Even as the Son of man came not to be ministered unto, but to minister, and to give his life a ransom for many" (Matt. 20:28). In the upper room, when

His disciples apparently refused to minister, Jesus arose, laid aside His outer garments, put on the long linen towel, and *washed their feet* (John 13). He took the place of a menial slave. This was the submissive mind in action—and no wonder Jesus experienced such joy!

During the American Civil War, General George B. McClellan was put in charge of the great army of the Potomac, mainly because public opinion was on his side. He fancied himself to be a great military leader and enjoyed hearing the people call him "a young Napoleon." However, his performance was less than sensational. President Lincoln commissioned him general-in-chief, hoping this would get some action, but still he procrastinated. One evening, Lincoln and two of his staff members went to visit McClellan, only to learn that he was at a wedding. The three men sat down to wait, and an hour later the general arrived home. Without paying any attention to the president, McClellan went upstairs and did not return. Half an hour later, Lincoln sent the servant to tell McClellan that the men were waiting. The servant came back to report that McClellan had gone to bed!

His associates angry, Lincoln merely got up and led the way home. "This is no time to be making points of etiquette and personal dignity," the president explained. "I would hold McClellan's horse if he will only bring us success." This attitude of humility was what helped to make Lincoln a great man and a great president. He was not thinking of himself; he was thinking of serving others. Service is the second mark of the submissive mind.

3. HE SACRIFICES (2:8)

Many people are willing to serve others *if* it does not cost them anything. But if there is a price to pay, they suddenly lose interest. Jesus "became obedient unto death, even the death of the cross" (Phil. 2:8). His was not the death of a martyr but the death of a Savior. He willingly laid down His life for the sins of the world.

Dr. J. H. Jowett said, "Ministry that costs nothing accomplishes nothing." If there is to be any blessing, there must be some "bleeding." At a religious festival in Brazil, a missionary was going from booth to booth, examining the wares. He saw a sign above one booth: "Cheap Crosses." He thought, "That's what many Christians are looking for these days—cheap crosses. My Lord's cross was not cheap. Why should mine be?"

The person with the submissive mind does not avoid sacrifice. He lives for the glory of God and the good of others, and if paying a price will honor Christ and help others, he is willing to do it. This was Paul's attitude (Phil. 2:17), Timothy's (Phil. 2:20), and also Epaphroditus's (Phil. 2:30). Sacrifice and service go together if service is to be true Christian ministry.

In his book *Dedication and Leadership,* Douglas Hyde explained how the Communists succeeded in their program. A member of the Communist Party himself for twenty years, Hyde understands their philosophy. He pointed out that the Communists never ask a man to do a "mean, little job." They always ask him boldly to undertake something that will cost him. They make big demands, and they get a ready response. Mr. Hyde called "the willingness to sacrifice" one of the most important factors in the success of the Communist program. Even the youths in the movement are expected to study, serve, give, and obey, and this is what attracts and holds them.

A church council was planning the annual Youth Sunday program, and one of the members suggested that the teenagers serve as ushers, lead in prayer, bring special music. One of the teens stood up and said, "Quite frankly, we're tired of being asked to do little things. We'd like to do something difficult this year, and maybe keep it going all year long. The kids have talked and prayed about this, and we'd like to work with our trustees in remodeling that basement room so it can be used for a classroom. And we'd like to start visiting our elderly members each week and taking them recordings of the services. And, if it's OK, we'd like to have a weekly witness on Sunday afternoons in the park. We hope this is OK with you."

He sat down, and the new youth pastor smiled to himself. He had privately challenged the teens to do something that would cost them—and they enthusiastically responded to the challenge. He knew that sacrifice is necessary if there is going to be true growth and ministry.

The test of the submissive mind is not just how much we are willing to take in terms of suffering, but how much we are willing to give in terms of sacrifice. One pastor complained that his men were changing the words of the hymn from "Take my life and let it be" to "Take my wife and let me be!" They were willing for others to make the sacrifices, but they were unwilling to sacrifice for others.

It is one of the paradoxes of the Christian life that the more we give, the more we receive; the more we sacrifice, the more God blesses. This is why the submissive mind leads to joy; it makes us more like Christ. This means sharing His joy as we also share in His sufferings. Of course, when love is the motive (Phil. 2:1), sacrifice is never measured or mentioned. The person who constantly talks about his sacrifices does not have the submissive mind.

Is it costing *you* anything to be a Christian?

4. HE GLORIFIES GOD (2:9–11)

This, of course, is the great goal of all that we do—to glorify God. Paul warns us against "vainglory" in Philippians 2:3. The kind of rivalry that pits Christian against Christian and ministry against ministry is not spiritual, nor is it satisfying. It is vain, empty. Jesus humbled Himself for others, and God highly exalted Him; the result of this exaltation is glory to God.

Our Lord's exaltation began with His resurrection. When men buried the body of Jesus, that was the last thing any human hands did to Him. From that point on, it was God who worked. Men had done their worst to the Savior, but God exalted Him and honored Him. Men gave Him names of ridicule and slander, but the Father gave Him a glorious name! Just as in His humiliation He was given the name "Jesus" (Matt. 1:21), so in His exaltation He was given the name "Lord" (Phil. 2:11; see Acts 2:32–36). He arose from the dead and then returned in victory to heaven, ascending to the Father's throne.

His exaltation included sovereign authority over all creatures in heaven, on earth, and under the earth. All will bow to Him (see Isa. 45:23). It is likely that the idea of "under the earth" refers to the lost, since God's family is either in heaven or on earth (Eph. 3:14–15). One day all will bow before Him and confess that He is Lord. Of course, it is possible for people to bow and confess *today,* and receive His gift of salvation (Rom. 10:9–10). To bow before Him now means salvation; to bow before Him at the judgment means condemnation.

The whole purpose of Christ's humiliation and exaltation is the glory of God (Phil. 2:11). As Jesus faced the cross, the glory of the Father was uppermost in His mind: "Father, the hour is come; glorify thy Son, that thy Son also may glorify thee" (John 17:1). In fact, He has given this glory to us (John 17:22), and one day we shall share it with Him in heaven (John 17:24; see Rom. 8:28–30). The work of salvation is much greater and grander than simply the salvation of a lost soul, as wonderful as that is. Our salvation has as its ultimate purpose the glory of God (Eph. 1:6, 12, 14).

The person with the submissive mind, as he lives for others, must expect sacrifice and service, but in the end, it is going to lead to glory. "Humble yourselves therefore under the mighty hand of God, that he may exalt you in due time" (1 Peter 5:6). Joseph suffered and served for thirteen years, but then God exalted him and made him the second ruler of Egypt. David was anointed king when he was but a youth. He experienced years of hardship and suffering, but at the right time, God exalted him as king of Israel.

The joy of the submissive mind comes not only from helping others and sharing in the fellowship of Christ's sufferings (Phil. 3:10), but primarily from the knowledge that we are glorifying God. We are letting our light shine through our good works, and this glorifies the Father in heaven (Matt. 5:16). We may not see the glory today, but we shall see it when Jesus comes and rewards His faithful servants.

QUESTIONS FOR PERSONAL REFLECTION
OR GROUP DISCUSSION

1. What is the difference between unity and uniformity?

2. What is true humility? How would you rate yourself in this area? What can you do practically to become more humble in your everyday life?

3. Why does selfishness never bring joy?

4. Why is pride the great enemy of the spiritual life?

5. In what ways did Jesus serve others? How do you think this affected what Jesus thought of Himself?

6. "Ministry that costs nothing accomplishes nothing." What does that statement mean to you?

7. "The more Christians give, the more they receive." Do you agree? Give some examples.

8. What does Jesus' life teach Christians about demanding their rights?

9. What was the whole purpose of Christ's humiliation and exaltation?

10. If we asked ourselves, "What would Jesus do?" every time we had a choice to make, how would Christians today impact their world? How might your life look different if you did this?

Chapter Six

THE INS AND OUTS OF CHRISTIAN LIVING

(Philippians 2:12–18)

Few things are harder to put up with," wrote Mark Twain, "than the annoyance of a good example." Perhaps the thing most annoying about a good example is its inability to accomplish the same achievements in our own lives. Admiration for a great person can inspire us, but it cannot enable us. Unless the person can enter into our own lives and share his skills, we cannot attain to his heights of accomplishment. It takes more than an example on the outside; it takes power on the inside.

Paul has just presented Jesus Christ as our great Example in the exercise of the submissive mind. We read it, and we agree with it, *but how do we go about practicing it?* How could any mortal man ever hope to achieve what Jesus Christ achieved? It seems almost presumptuous to even try! Here we are, trying to develop humility, and we are exercising pride by daring to imitate the Lord Jesus Christ.

The problem is really not that difficult. Paul was not asking us to "reach for the stars," though the higher the goal the more we ought to achieve. Rather, he was setting before us the divine *pattern* for the submissive mind and the divine *power* to accomplish what God has commanded. "It is God which worketh in you" (Phil. 2:13). It is not by imitation, but by incarnation—"Christ liveth in me" (Gal. 2:20). The Christian life is not a series of ups and downs. It is rather a process of "ins and outs." God works *in,* and we work *out.* We cultivate the submissive mind by responding to the divine provisions God makes available to us.

THERE IS A PURPOSE TO ACHIEVE (2:12, 14–16)

"Work out your own salvation" (Phil. 2:12) does not suggest, "Work *for* your own salvation." To begin with, Paul was writing to people who were already "saints" (Phil. 1:1), which means they had trusted Christ and had been set apart for Him. The verb "work out" carries the meaning of "work to full completion," such as working out a problem in mathematics. In Paul's day it was also used for "working a mine," that is, getting out of the mine all the valuable ore possible; or "working a field" so as to get the greatest harvest possible. The purpose God wants us to achieve is Christlikeness, "to be conformed to the image of his Son" (Rom. 8:29). There are problems in life, but God will help us to "work them out." Our lives have tremendous potential, like a mine or a field, and He wants to help us fulfill that potential.

Cindy did not seem very happy when she arrived home from college to spend the holiday with her family. Her parents noticed her unusual behavior but were wise enough to wait until she was ready to share her problem with them. It happened after dinner.

"Mother, Dad, I have something to tell you, and I'm afraid it's going to hurt you."

"Just tell us what's on your heart," her father said, "and we'll understand. We want to pray with you about it—whatever it is."

"Well, you know that all during high school I talked about becoming a nurse, mainly because Mom is a nurse, and I guess you expected me to follow in her footsteps. But I can't go on. The Lord just doesn't want me to be a nurse!"

Her mother smiled and took Cindy's hand. "Dear, your father and I want God's will for your life. If you do anything else, we'll *all* be unhappy!"

Cindy had done the courageous thing; she had faced God's will and decided that she wanted to work out *her own salvation*—her own Christian life—and not what somebody else wanted her to do. One of the wonderful things about being a Christian is the knowledge that God has a plan for our lives (Eph. 2:10) and will help us to work it out for His glory. Our God is a God of infinite variety! No two flowers are the same, no two snowflakes are the same; why should two Christians be the same? All of us must be like Christ, *but we must also be ourselves.*

The phrase "work out your own salvation" probably has reference particularly to the special problems in the church at Philippi, but the statement also applies to the individual Christian. We are not to be "cheap imitations" of other people, especially "great Christians." We are to follow only what we see of Christ in their lives. "Be ye followers of me, even as I also am of Christ" (1 Cor. 11:1). Every "great saint" has feet of clay and ultimately may disappoint you, but Jesus Christ can never fail you.

In Philippians 2:14–15, Paul contrasted the life of the believer with the lives of those who live in the world. Unsaved people complain and find fault, but Christians rejoice. Society around us is twisted and distorted, but the Christian stands straight because he measures his life by God's Word, the perfect standard. The world is dark, but Christians shine as bright lights. The world has nothing to offer, but the Christian holds out the Word of life, the message of salvation through faith in Christ. In other words, as we allow God to achieve this purpose in our lives, we become better witnesses in a world that desperately needs Christ. Apply these characteristics to Jesus and you will see that He lived a perfect life in an imperfect world.

It is important to note that this purpose is achieved "in the midst of a crooked and perverse generation" (Phil. 2:15). Paul did not admonish us to retreat from the world and go into a spiritual isolation ward. It is only as we are confronted with the needs and problems of real life that we can begin to become more like Christ. The Pharisees were so isolated and insulated from reality that they developed an artificial kind of self-righteousness that was totally unlike the righteousness God wanted them to have. Consequently, the Pharisees forced a religion of fear and bondage on the people (read Matt. 23), and they crucified Christ because He dared to oppose that kind of religion. It is not by leaving the world but by ministering to it that we see God's purpose fulfilled in our lives.

THERE IS A POWER TO RECEIVE (2:13)

The principle Paul laid down is this: God must work *in* us before He can work *through* us. This principle is seen at work throughout the Bible in the lives of men like Moses, David, the apostles, and others. God had a special purpose for each man to fulfill, and each man was unique and not an imitation of somebody else. For example, it took God forty years to bring Moses to the place where He could use him to lead the people of Israel. As Moses tended sheep during those forty years, God was working in him so that one day He might work through him. *God is more interested in the workman than in the work.* If the workman is what he ought to be, the work will be what it ought to be.

Too many Christians obey God only because of pressure on the outside, and not power on the inside. Paul warned the Philippians that not his presence with them but their desire to obey God and please Him was the important thing (Phil. 1:27; 2:12). They could not build their lives on Paul because he might not be with them very long. It is sad to see the way some ministries in the church weaken or fall apart because of a change in leadership. We have a tendency to please men and to obey God only when others are watching. But when you surrender to the power of God within you, then obedience becomes a delight and not a battle.

The power that works in us is the power of the Holy Spirit of God (John 14:16–17, 26; Acts 1:8; 1 Cor. 6:19–20). Our English word *energy* comes from the word translated "worketh" in Philippians 2:13. It is God's divine energy at work in us and through us. The same Holy Spirit who empowered Christ when He was ministering on earth can empower us as well. But we must recognize the fact that the energy of the flesh (Rom. 7:5) and of the Devil (Eph. 2:2; 2 Thess. 2:7) are also at work. Because of the death, resurrection, and ascension of Christ, God's divine energy is available to us (Eph. 1:18–23). The power is here, but how do we use it? What "tools" does God use, by His Spirit, to work in our lives? There are three tools: the Word of God, prayer, and suffering.

(1) The Word of God. "For this cause also thank we God without ceasing, because, when ye received the word of God, which ye heard of us, ye received it not as the word of men, but as it is in truth, the word of God, which effectually worketh also in you that believe" (1 Thess. 2:13). God's divine energy is released in our lives through His inspired Word. The same Word that spoke the universe into being can release divine power in our lives. But we have a responsibility to *appreciate* the Word, and not treat it the way we treat the words of men. The Word of God is unique: it is inspired, authoritative, and infallible. If we do not appreciate the Word, then God's power cannot energize our lives.

But we must also *appropriate* the Word—"receive it." This means much more than listening to it, or even reading and studying it. To "receive" God's Word means to welcome it and make it a part of our inner being. God's truth is to the spiritual man what food is to the physical man.

Finally, we must *apply* the Word; it works only in those who believe. When we trust God's Word and act on it, then God's power is released in our lives. The angel's promise to Mary in Luke 1:37—"For with God nothing shall be impossible"—is translated "For no word from God shall be void of power" in the American Standard Version (1901). God's Word has the power of accomplishment in it, and faith releases that power.

We see this truth operating in the life of Jesus. He commanded the crippled man to stretch out his hand, and the very command gave him the power to obey and be healed (Matt. 12:13). He commanded Peter to walk to Him on the water, and the command enabled Peter to do so, as long as he exercised faith (Matt. 14:22–33). It is faith in God's promises that releases God's power. His commandments are His enablements. The Holy Spirit wrote down the promises for us in the Word, and He gives us the faith to lay hold of these promises. "For no matter how many promises God has made, they are 'Yes' in Christ. And so through him the 'Amen' is spoken by us to the glory of God" (2 Cor. 1:20 NIV).

(2) Prayer. *So* if we want God's power working in us, we must spend time daily with the Word of God. But we must also pray, because *prayer* is the second tool God uses to work in the lives of His children. "Now unto him that is able to do exceeding abundantly above all that we ask or think, according to the power that worketh in us" (Eph. 3:20). The Holy Spirit is closely related to the practice of prayer in our lives (Rom. 8:26–27; Zech. 12:10). The book of Acts makes it clear that prayer is a divinely ordained source of spiritual power (Acts 1:14; 4:23–31; 12:5, 12), and the Word of God and prayer go together (Acts 6:4). Unless the Christian takes time for prayer, God cannot work in him and through him. In the Bible and in church history, the people God used were people who prayed.

(3) Suffering. God's third tool is *suffering*. The Spirit of God works in a special way in the lives of those who suffer for the glory of Christ (1 Peter 4:12–19). The "fiery trial" has a way of burning away the dross and empowering the believer to serve Christ. Paul himself had experienced God's power in that Philippian jail when he was beaten and thrust into the stocks in the inner prison, for he was able to sing and praise God in spite of his suffering (Acts 16:19–33). His "fiery trial" also enabled him to forgive the jailer. It was not the earthquake that brought conviction to the man; the earthquake almost led him to suicide! It was Paul's encouraging word, "Don't do it! We are all here!" (TLB). This kind of love broke the man's heart, and he fell before Paul asking how to be saved.

The Word of God, prayer, and suffering are the three tools that God uses in our lives. Just as electricity must run through a conductor, so the Holy Spirit must work through the means God has provided. As the Christian reads the Word and prays, he becomes more like Christ, and the more he becomes like Christ, the more the unsaved world opposes him. This daily "fellowship of his sufferings" (Phil. 3:10) drives the believer back to the Word and prayer, so that all three tools work together to provide the spiritual power he needs to glorify Christ.

If we are to have the submissive mind, and the joy that goes with it, we must recognize that there is a purpose to achieve (God's plan for our lives), a power to receive (the Holy Spirit), and a promise to believe.

THERE IS A PROMISE TO BELIEVE (2:16–18)

What is this promise? *That joy comes from submission.* The world's philosophy is that joy comes from aggression: fight everybody to get what you want, and you will get it and be happy. The example of Jesus is proof enough that the world's philosophy is wrong. He never used a sword or any other weapon, yet He won the greatest battle in history—the battle against sin and death and hell. He defeated hatred by manifesting love; He overcame lies with truth. *Because He surrendered He was victorious!* And you and I must dare to believe His promise, "For whosoever exalteth himself shall be abased; and he that humbleth himself shall be exalted" (Luke 14:11). "How happy are the humble-minded, for the kingdom of heaven is theirs" (Matt. 5:3 PH).

There is a twofold joy that comes to the person who possesses and practices the submissive mind: a joy hereafter (Phil. 2:16) and a joy here and now (Phil. 2:17–18). In the day of Christ (see Phil. 1:10), God is going to reward those who have been faithful to Him. "The joy of thy Lord" is going to be a part of that reward (Matt. 25:21). The faithful Christian will discover that his sufferings on earth have been transformed into glory in heaven. He will see that his work was not in vain (1 Cor. 15:58). It was this same kind of promise of future joy that helped our Savior in His sufferings on the cross (Heb. 12:1–2).

But we do not have to wait for the return of Christ to start experiencing the joy of the submissive mind. That joy is a present reality (Phil. 2:17–18), and it comes through sacrifice and service. It is remarkable that in two verses that discuss sacrifice, Paul used the words *joy* and *rejoice*— and repeats them! Most people would associate sorrow with suffering, but Paul saw suffering and sacrifice as doorways to a deeper joy in Christ.

In Philippians 2:17, Paul was comparing his experience of sacrifice to that of the priest pouring out the drink offering (Num. 15:1–10). It was possible that Paul's trial would go against him and he would be executed. But this did not rob Paul of his joy. His death would be a willing sacrifice, a priestly ministry, on behalf of Christ and His church, and this would give him joy. Sacrifice and service are marks of the submissive mind (Phil. 2:7–8, 21–22, 30), and the submissive mind experiences joy even in the midst of suffering.

It takes faith to exercise the submissive mind. We must believe that God's promises are true and that they are going to work in our lives just as they worked in Paul's life. God works *in* us through the Word, prayer, and suffering, and we work *out* in daily living and service. God fulfills His purposes in us as we receive and believe His Word. Life is not a series of disappointing ups and downs. Rather, it is a sequence of delightful ins and outs. God works in—we work out. The example comes from Christ, the energy comes from the Holy Spirit, and the result is—JOY!

QUESTIONS FOR PERSONAL REFLECTION
OR GROUP DISCUSSION

1. What does it mean to "work out your own salvation"? What does this look like in your own life?

2. Do you think most Christians obey Philippians 2:14–15 as they should? Why or why not?

3. How can Christians be bright lights in a dark world?

4. "God must work in us before He can work through us." What does that statement mean to you?

5. Do you think God is more interested in the workman than in the work? Why or why not?

6. What part does the Holy Spirit play in the Christian's accomplishments for God?

7. What are the three tools God uses to work in our lives?

8. How has God used these tools in your life? How can you improve in these areas?

9. What is the difference between the world's philosophy of joy and the Christian's?

10. "God works in—we work out." What does that mean in your everyday Christian life?

Chapter Seven

A PRICELESS PAIR

(Philippians 2:19–30)

A reporter in San Bernardino, California, arranged for a man to lie in the gutter on a busy street. Hundreds of people passed the man, but not one stopped to help him or even show sympathy.

Newspapers across the country some years ago told how thirty-eight people watched a man stalk a young woman and finally attack her—and none of the spectators even picked up a phone to call the police!

A couple of teenagers in Detroit discovered a woman in a telephone booth who had suffered a heart attack. They carried her to a nearby house and rang the bell, asking for help. The only reply they received was, "Get off my porch—and take her with you!"

A Kentucky doctor was driving down the highway to visit a patient when he saw an accident take place. He stopped and gave aid to the injured and then made his visit. One of the drivers he helped sued him.

Is it possible to be a Good Samaritan today? Must everybody harden his heart in order to protect himself? Perhaps sacrifice and service are ancient virtues that somehow do not fit into our so-called modern civilization. It is worth noting that even in Paul's day mutual concern was not a popular virtue. The Christians at Rome were not too interested in the problems at

Philippi; Paul could not find *one person* among them willing to go to Philippi (Phil. 2:19–21). Times have not changed too much.

In this paragraph, Paul was still discussing the submissive mind. He has given us a *description* of the submissive mind in the example of Jesus Christ (Phil. 2:1–11). He has explained the *dynamics* of the submissive mind in his own experience (Phil. 2:12–18). Next he introduced us to two of his helpers in the ministry, Timothy and Epaphroditus, and he did this for a reason. He knew that his readers would be prone to say, "It is impossible for us to follow such examples as Christ and Paul! After all, Jesus is the very Son of God, and Paul is a chosen apostle who has had great spiritual experiences!" For this reason, Paul introduced us to two ordinary saints, men who were not apostles or spectacular miracle workers. He wanted us to know that the submissive mind is not a luxury enjoyed by a chosen few; it is a necessity for Christian joy, and an opportunity for *all* believers.

TIMOTHY (PHIL. 2:19–24)

Paul probably met Timothy on his first missionary journey (Acts 14:6ff.), at which time, perhaps, the youth was converted (1 Cor. 4:17). Apparently, Timothy's mother and grandmother had been converted first (2 Tim. 1:5). He was the son of a Jewish mother and Gentile father, but Paul always considered the young man his own "dearly beloved son" in the faith (2 Tim. 1:2). When Paul returned to Derbe and Lystra while on his second journey, he enlisted young Timothy as one of his fellow laborers (Acts 16:1–4). In one sense, Timothy replaced John Mark, whom Paul had refused to take along on the journey because of Mark's previous abandonment of the cause (Acts 13:13; 15:36–41).

In Timothy's experience, we learn that the submissive mind is not something that suddenly, automatically appears in the life of the believer. Timothy had to develop and cultivate the "mind of Christ." It was not natural for him to be a servant; but, as he walked with the Lord and worked with Paul, he became the kind of servant that Paul could trust and God could bless. Notice the characteristics of this young man.

He had a servant's mind (vv. 19–21). To begin with, Timothy naturally cared for people and was concerned about their needs. He was not interested in "winning friends and influencing people"; he was genuinely interested in their physical and spiritual welfare. Paul was concerned about the church at Philippi and wanted to send someone to convey his concern and get the facts. There were certainly hundreds of Christians in Rome (Paul greeted twenty-six of them by name in Rom. 16); yet not one of them was available to make the trip! "All seek their own, not the things which are Jesus Christ's" (Phil. 2:21). In a very real sense, all of us live either in Philippians 1:21 or Philippians 2:21!

But Timothy had a natural concern for the welfare of others; he had a servant's mind. It is too bad that the believers in Rome were so engrossed in themselves and their own internal wranglings (Phil. 1:15–16) that they had no time for the important work of the Lord. This is one of the tragedies of church problems; they divert time, energy, and concern away from the things that matter most. Timothy was not interested in promoting any party or supporting any divisive cause. He was interested only in the spiritual condition of God's people, and this concern was *natural* to him. How did this concern develop? The answer is in the next characteristic of this remarkable young man.

He had a servant's training (v. 22). Paul did not add Timothy to his "team" the very day the boy was saved. Paul was too wise to make an error like that. He left him behind to become a part of the church fellowship in Derbe and Lystra, and it was in that fellowship that Timothy grew in spiritual matters and learned how to serve the Lord. When Paul returned to that area a few years later, he was happy to discover that young Timothy "was well reported of the brethren" (Acts 16:2). Years later, Paul would write to Timothy about the importance of permitting new converts to grow before thrusting them into important places of ministry (1 Tim. 3:6–7).

A popular local nightclub performer visited a pastor and announced that he had been saved and wanted to serve the Lord. "What should I do next?" he asked.

"Well, I'd suggest you unite with a good church and start growing," the pastor replied. "Is your wife a Christian?"

"No, she isn't," the musician replied. "I hope to win her. But do I have to wait? I mean, I'd like to do something for God right now."

"No, you don't have to wait to witness for the Lord," explained the pastor. "Get busy in a church, and use your talents for Christ."

"But you don't know who I am!" the man protested. "I'm a big performer—everybody knows me. I want to start my own organization, make records, and appear before big crowds!"

"If you go too far too fast," warned the pastor, "you may hurt yourself and your testimony. And the place to start winning people is right at home. God will open up places of service for you as He sees you are ready. Meanwhile, study the Bible and give yourself a chance to grow."

The man did not take the pastor's counsel. Instead, he set up a big organization and started out on his own. His "success" lasted less than a year. Not only did he lose his testimony because he was not strong enough to carry the heavy burdens, but his constant traveling alienated him from his wife and family. He drifted into a fringe group and disappeared from public ministry, a broken and bankrupt man.

"His branches went out farther than his roots went deep," the pastor said. "When that happens, you eventually topple."

Paul did not make this mistake with Timothy. He gave him time to get his roots down, and then he enlisted the young man to work with him on his missionary tours. He taught Timothy the Word and permitted him to watch the apostle in his ministry (2 Tim. 3:10–17). This was the way Jesus trained His disciples. He gave personal instruction balanced by on-the-job experience. Experience without teaching can lead to discouragement, and teaching without experience can lead to spiritual deadness. It takes both.

He had a servant's reward (vv. 23–24). Timothy knew the meaning of "sacrifice and service" (Phil. 2:17), but God rewarded him for his faithfulness. To begin with, Timothy had the joy of helping others. To be sure, there were hardships and difficulties, but there were also victories and blessings. Because Timothy was a "good and faithful servant," "faithful over a few things," God rewarded him with "many things," and he entered into the joy of the submissive mind (Matt. 25:21). He had the joy of serving with the great apostle Paul and assisting him in some of his most difficult assignments (1 Cor. 4:17ff.; Timothy is mentioned at least twenty-four times in Paul's letters).

But perhaps the greatest reward God gave to Timothy was to choose him to be Paul's replacement when the great apostle was called home (see 2 Tim. 4:1–11). Paul himself wanted to go to Philippi, but had had to send Timothy in his place. But what an honor! Timothy was not only Paul's son and Paul's servant, but he became Paul's substitute. His name is held in high regard by Christians today, something that young Timothy never dreamed of when he was busy serving Christ.

The submissive mind is not the product of an hour's sermon, or a week's seminar, or even a year's service. The submissive mind grows in us as, like Timothy, we yield to the Lord and seek to serve others.

EPAPHRODITUS (2:25–30)

Paul was a "Hebrew of the Hebrews"; Timothy was part Jew and part Gentile (Acts 16:1); and Epaphroditus was a full Gentile as far as we know. He was the member of the Philippian church who risked his health and life to carry their missionary offering to the apostle in Rome (Phil. 4:18). His name means "charming," and a charming Christian he is!

He was a balanced Christian (v. 25). Paul could not say enough about this man—"my brother, and companion in labour, and fellow soldier." These three descriptions parallel what Paul wrote about the gospel in the first chapter of this letter:

"my brother"	the "fellowship in the gospel" (Phil. 1:5)
"my companion in labour"	"the furtherance of the gospel" (Phil. 1:12)
"my fellow soldier"	"the faith of the gospel" (Phil. 1:27)

Epaphroditus was a balanced Christian!

Balance is important in the Christian life. Some people emphasize "fellowship" so much that they forget "the furtherance of the gospel." Others are so involved in defending the "faith of the gospel" that they neglect building fellowship with other believers. Epaphroditus did not fall into either of these traps. He was like Nehemiah, the man who rebuilt the walls of Jerusalem with his sword in one hand and his trowel in the other (Neh. 4:17). You cannot build with a sword nor battle with a trowel! It takes both to get the Lord's work accomplished.

Dr. H. A. Ironside used to tell about a group of believers who thought only of fellowship. They had little concern for reaching the lost or for defending the faith against its enemies. In front of their meeting place they hung a sign that read JESUS ONLY. But the wind blew away some of the letters, and the sign read US ONLY. It was a perfect description of a group of people who were not balanced Christians.

He was a burdened Christian (vv. 26–27, 30). Like Timothy, Epaphroditus was concerned about others. To begin with, he was concerned about *Paul*. When he heard in Philippi that Paul was a prisoner in Rome, he volunteered to make that long, dangerous trip to Rome to stand at Paul's side and assist him. He carried the church's love gift with him, protecting it with his own life.

Our churches today need men and women who are burdened for missions and for those in difficult places of Christian service. "The problem in our churches," states one missionary leader, "is that we have too many spectators and not enough participants." Epaphroditus was not content simply to contribute to the offering. He gave *himself to* help carry the offering!

But this man was also burdened for *his own home church*. After arriving in Rome, he became very ill. In fact, he almost died. This delayed his return to Philippi, and the people there became concerned about him. But Epaphroditus was not burdened about himself; he was burdened over the people in Philippi *because they were worried about him*. This man lived in Philippians 1:21, not Philippians 2:21. Like Timothy, he had a natural concern for others. The phrase "full of heaviness" in Philippines 2:26 is the same description used of Christ in Gethsemane (Matt. 26:37). Like Christ, Epaphroditus knew the meaning of sacrifice and service (Phil. 2:30), which are two of the marks of the submissive mind.

He was a blessed Christian (vv. 28–30). What a tragedy it would be to go through life and not be a blessing to anyone! Epaphroditus was a blessing to Paul. He stood with him in his prison experience and did not permit even his own sickness to hinder his service. What times he and Paul must have had together! But he was also a blessing to his own church. Paul admonished the church to honor him because of his sacrifice and service. (Christ gets the glory, but there is nothing wrong with the servant receiving honor. Read 1 Thess. 5:12–13.) There is no contradiction between

Philippians 2:7 ("made himself of no reputation") and Philippians 2:29 ("hold such in reputation"). Christ "emptied Himself" in His gracious act of humiliation, and God exalted Him. Epaphroditus sacrificed himself with no thought of reward, and Paul encouraged the church to hold him in honor to the glory of God.

He was a blessing to Paul and to his own church, and he is also a blessing to us *today.* He proves to us that the joyful life is the life of sacrifice and service, that the submissive mind really does work. He and Timothy together encourage us to submit ourselves to the Lord, and to one another, in the Spirit of Christ. Christ is the pattern we follow. Paul shows us the power (Phil. 4:12–19), and Timothy and Epaphroditus are the proof that this mind really works.

Will you permit the Spirit to reproduce "the mind of Christ" in you?

QUESTIONS FOR PERSONAL REFLECTION
OR GROUP DISCUSSION

1. What are some of the more reasonable excuses people give for not helping others?

2. Why do such reasonable excuses really not excuse us?

3. What are the real reasons we fail to help others?

4. What does the author mean when he says "all of us live either in Philippians 1:21 or Philippians 2:21"?

5. Why are both experience and teaching necessary in a Christian's training to serve the Lord?

6. How was Timothy rewarded and blessed on earth, in addition to the heavenly reward waiting for him?

7. Have you known balanced Christians like Epaphroditus? Explain what effect they had on you.

8. Why is fellowship so important in the church? Can it become too important?

9. Do you agree that we have "too many spectators and not enough participants" in the church today? Explain.

10. A popular Christian song says that we are "blessed to be a blessing." What does that mean to you?

Chapter Eight

LEARNING HOW TO COUNT

(Philippians 3:1–11)

C ircumstances and people can rob us of joy, but so can *things,* and it is this "thief" that Paul deals with in Philippians 3. It is important to see the total message of this chapter before examining it in detail, so perhaps the following outline will be helpful.

vv. 1–11	*vv. 12–16*	*vv. 17–21*
Paul's past	Paul's present	Paul's future
the accountant	the athlete	the alien
"I count"	"I press"	"I look"
new values	new vigor	new vision

What Paul was describing is the "spiritual mind." In Philippians 3:18–19, he described professed Christians who "mind earthly things," but then in Philippians 3:20 he described the believer with the spiritual mind, who minds heavenly things. You will recall that the city of Philippi was actually a Roman colony—a "Rome away from Rome." In the same sense, the people of God are a colony of heaven on earth. "Our citizenship is in heaven" (Phil. 3:20 NASB), and we look at earth from heaven's point of view. This is the spiritual mind.

It is easy for us to get wrapped up in "things," not only the tangible things that we can see, but also the intangibles such as reputation, fame, achievement. Paul wrote about "what things were gain" to him (Phil. 3:7); he also mentioned "things which are behind" and "things which are before" (Phil. 3:13). In Paul's case, some of these "things" were intangible, such as religious achievements (Gal. 1:14), a feeling of self-satisfaction, morality. We today can be snared both by tangibles and intangibles, and as a result lose our joy.

But even the tangible things are not in themselves sinful. God made things, and the Bible declares that these things are good (Gen. 1:31). God knows that we need certain things in order to live (Matt. 6:31–34). In fact, He "giveth us richly all things to enjoy" (1 Tim. 6:17). But Jesus warned us that our lives do not consist in the abundance of the things that we possess (Luke 12:15). Quantity is no assurance of quality. Many people who have the things money can buy have lost the things that money cannot buy.

The key word in Philippians 3:1–11 is *count* (Phil. 3:7–8). In the Greek, two different words are used, but the basic idea is the same: to evaluate, to assess. "The unexamined life is not worth living," Socrates said. Yet few people sit down to weigh seriously the values that control their decisions and directions. Many people today are the slaves of "things," and as a result do not experience real Christian joy.

In Paul's case, the "things" he was living for before he knew Christ seemed to be very commendable: a righteous life, obedience to the law, the defense of the religion of his fathers. But none of these things satisfied him or gave him acceptance with God.

Like most religious people today, Paul had enough morality to keep him out of trouble, but not enough righteousness to get him into heaven. It was not bad things that kept Paul away from Jesus—it was good things. He had to lose his religion to find salvation.

One day Saul of Tarsus, the rabbi, met Jesus Christ, the Son of God, and on that day Saul's values changed (read Acts 9:1–31). When Saul opened his books to evaluate his wealth, he discovered that apart from Jesus Christ, everything he lived for was only refuse. He explained in this section that there are only two kinds of righteousness (or spiritual wealth)—works righteousness and faith righteousness—and only faith righteousness is acceptable to God.

WORKS RIGHTEOUSNESS (3:1–6)

The exhortation (vv. 1–3). "Finally" at this point does not mean Paul is about to close the letter, because he keeps on going. The word means "For the rest," and introduces the new section. Paul's "finally" at Philippians 4:8 is the one that means "I am about to close." Paul has warned the believers at Philippi before, but now he warned them again. "Look out for dogs! Look out for the workers of evil! Look out for the mutilation!" To whom was he referring in this triple warning? The answer takes us back into the early history of the church.

From the very beginning, the gospel came "to the Jew first" (see Acts 3:26; Rom. 1:16), so that the first seven chapters of Acts deal only with Jewish believers or with Gentiles who were Jewish proselytes (Acts 2:10). In Acts 8:5–25, the message went to the Samaritans, but this did not cause too much of an upheaval since the Samaritans were at least partly Jewish. But when Peter went to the Gentiles in Acts 10, this created an uproar. Peter was called on the carpet to explain his activities (Acts 11). After all, the Gentiles in Acts 10 had become Christians *without first becoming Jews,* and this was a whole new thing for the church. Peter explained that it was God who had directed him to preach to the Gentiles, and the matter seemed to be settled.

But it was not settled for long. Paul was sent out by the Holy Spirit to minister especially to the Gentiles (Acts 13:1–3; 22:21). Peter had opened the door of faith to the Gentiles in Acts 10, and Paul followed his example on his first missionary journey (see Acts 14:26–28). It did not take long for the strict Jewish believers to oppose Paul's ministry and come to Antioch teaching that it was necessary for the Gentiles to submit to Jewish rules before they could be saved (Acts 15:1). This disagreement led to the Conference at Jerusalem that is described in Acts 15. The result of the conference was an approval of Paul's ministry and a victory for the gospel of the grace of God. Gentiles did *not* have to become Jewish proselytes in order to become Christians.

But the dissenters were not content. Having failed in their opposition to Paul at Antioch and Jerusalem, they followed him wherever he went and tried to steal his converts and his churches. Bible students call this group of false teachers who try to mix law and grace Judaizers. The epistle to the Galatians was written primarily to combat this false teaching. It is this group of Judaizers that Paul was referring to in Philippians 3:1–2. He used three terms to describe them.

"Dogs." The orthodox Jew would call the Gentile a dog, but here Paul called orthodox Jews "dogs"! Paul was not just using names; he was comparing these false teachers to the dirty scavengers so contemptible to decent people. Like those dogs, these Judaizers snapped at Paul's heels and followed him from place to place "barking" their false doctrines. They were troublemakers and carriers of dangerous infection.

"Evil workers." These men taught that the sinner was saved by faith *plus* good works, especially the works of the law. But Paul stated that their good works are really *evil* works because they are performed by the flesh (old nature) and not the Spirit, and they glorify the workers and not Jesus Christ. Ephesians 2:8–10 and Titus 3:3–7 make it clear that nobody can be saved by doing good works, even religious works. A Christian's good works are the result of his faith, not the basis for his salvation.

"The mutilation." Here Paul used a pun on the word *circumcision*. The word translated "circumcision" literally means "a mutilation." The Judaizers taught that circumcision was essential to salvation (Acts 15:1; Gal. 6:12–18), but Paul stated that circumcision of *itself* is only a mutilation. The true Christian has experienced a spiritual circumcision in Christ (Col. 2:11), and does not need any fleshly operations. Circumcision, baptism, the Lord's supper, tithing, or any other religious practice cannot save a person from his sins. Only faith in Jesus Christ can do that.

In contrast to the false Christians, Paul described the true Christians, the "true circumcision" (see Rom. 2:25–29 for a parallel).

He worships God in the Spirit. He does not depend on his own good works, which are only of the flesh (see John 4:19–24).

He boasts in Jesus Christ. People who depend on religion are usually boasting about what they have done. The true Christian has nothing of which to boast (Eph. 2:8–10). His boast is only in Christ! In Luke 18:9–14, Jesus gave a parable that describes these two opposite attitudes.

He has no confidence in the flesh. The popular religious philosophy of today is "The Lord helps those who help themselves." It was also popular in Paul's day, and it is just as wrong today as it was then. (By "the flesh" Paul meant "the old nature" that we received at birth.) The Bible has nothing good to say about flesh, and yet most people today depend entirely on what they themselves can do to please God. Flesh only corrupts God's way on earth (Gen. 6:12). It profits nothing as far as spiritual life is concerned (John 6:63). It has nothing good in it (Rom. 7:18). No wonder we should put no confidence in the flesh!

A woman was arguing with her pastor about this matter of faith and works. "I think that getting to heaven is like rowing a boat," she said. "One oar is faith, and the other is works. If you use both, you get there. If you use only one, you go around in circles."

"There is only one thing wrong with your illustration," replied the pastor. "Nobody is going to heaven *in a rowboat!*"

There is only one good work that takes the sinner to heaven: the finished work of Christ on the cross (John 17:1–4; 19:30; Heb. 10:11–14).

The example (vv. 4–6). Paul was not speaking from an ivory tower; he personally *knew* the futility of trying to attain salvation by means of good works. As a young student, he had sat at the feet of Gamaliel, the great rabbi (Acts 22:3). His career as a Jewish religious leader was a promising one (Gal. 1:13–14), and yet Paul gave it all up—to become a hated member of the "Christian sect" and a preacher of the gospel. Actually, the Judaizers were compromising in order to avoid persecution (Gal. 6:12–13), while Paul was being true to Christ's message of grace and as a result was suffering persecution.

In this intensely autobiographical section, Paul examined his own life. He became an auditor who opens the books to see what wealth he has, and he discovers that *he is bankrupt.*

Paul's relationship to the nation. He was born into a pure Hebrew family and entered into a covenantal relationship when he was circumcised. He was not a proselyte, nor was he descended from Ishmael (Abraham's other son) or Esau (Isaac's other son). The Judaizers would understand Paul's reference to the tribe of Benjamin, because Benjamin and Joseph were Jacob's favorite sons. They were born to Rachel, Jacob's favorite wife. Israel's first king came from Benjamin, and this little tribe was faithful to David during the rebellion under Absalom. Paul's human heritage was something to be proud of. When measured by this standard, he passed with flying colors.

Paul's relationship to the law. "As touching the law, a Pharisee ... touching the righteousness which is in the law, blameless" (Phil. 3:5–6). To the Jews of Paul's day, a Pharisee had reached the very summit of religious experience, the highest ideal a Jew could ever hope to attain. If anybody was going to heaven, it was the Pharisee. He held to orthodox doctrine (see Acts 23:6–9) and tried to fulfill the religious duties faithfully (Luke 18:10–14). While we today are accustomed to use the word *Pharisee* as the equivalent of "hypocrite," this usage was not prevalent in Paul's day. Measured by the righteousness of the law, Paul was blameless. He kept the law and the traditions perfectly.

Paul's relationship to Israel's enemies. But it is not enough to believe the truth; a man must also oppose lies. Paul defended his orthodox faith by persecuting the followers of "that deceiver," Jesus (Matt. 27:62–66). He assisted at the stoning of Stephen (Acts 7:54–60), and after that he led the attack against the church in general (Acts 8:1–3). Even in later years, Paul admitted his role in persecuting the church (Acts 22:1–5; 26:1–11; see also 1 Tim. 1:12–16). Every Jew could boast of his own blood heritage (though he certainly could not take any credit for it). Some Jews could boast of their faithfulness to the Jewish religion. But Paul could boast of those things *plus* his zeal in persecuting the church.

At this point we might ask, "How could a sincere man like Saul of Tarsus be so wrong?" The answer is, *he was using the wrong measuring stick!* Like the rich young ruler (Mark 10:17–22) and the Pharisee in Christ's parable (Luke 18:10–14), Saul of Tarsus was looking at the *outside* and not the *inside*. He was comparing himself with standards set by men, not by God. As far as obeying *outwardly* the demands of the law was concerned, Paul was a success, but he did not stop to consider the *inward sins* he was committing. In the Sermon on the Mount, Jesus made it clear that there are sinful *attitudes* and *appetites* as well as sinful *actions* (Matt. 5:21–48).

When he looked at himself or looked at others, Saul of Tarsus considered himself to be righteous. But one day he saw himself as compared with Jesus Christ. It was then that he changed his evaluations and values, and abandoned "works righteousness" for the righteousness of Jesus Christ.

FAITH RIGHTEOUSNESS (3:7–11)

When Paul met Jesus Christ on the Damascus road (Acts 9), he trusted Him and became a child of God. It was an instantaneous miracle of the grace of God, the kind that still takes place today whenever sinners will admit their need and turn to the Savior by faith. When Paul met Christ, he realized how futile were his good works and how sinful were his claims of righteousness. A wonderful transaction took place. Paul lost some things, but he gained much more than he lost.

Paul's losses (v. 7). To begin with, he lost whatever was *gain to him personally apart from God.* Certainly Paul had a great reputation as a scholar (Acts 26:24) and a religious leader. He was proud of his Jewish heritage and his religious achievements. All of these things were valuable to him; he could profit from them. He certainly had many friends who admired his zeal. But he measured these treasures against what Jesus Christ had to offer, and he realized that all he held dear was really nothing but refuse compared to what he had in Christ. His own treasures brought glory to him personally, but they did not bring glory to God. They were "gain" to him only, and as such, were selfish.

This does not mean that Paul repudiated his rich heritage as an orthodox Jew. As you read his letters and follow his ministry in the book of Acts, you see how he valued both his Jewish blood and his Roman citizenship. Becoming a Christian did not make him *less* a Jew. In fact, it made him a *completed* Jew, a true child of Abraham both spiritually and physically (Gal. 3:6–9). Nor did he lower his standards of morality because he saw the shallowness of Pharisaical religion. He accepted the *higher* standard of living—conformity to Jesus Christ (Rom. 12:1–2). When a person becomes a Christian, God takes away the bad, but He also takes the good and makes it better.

Paul's gains (vv. 8–11). Again we are reminded of Jim Elliot's words:

"He is no fool who gives what he cannot keep to gain that which he can-not lose." This is what Paul experienced: He lost his religion and his reputation, but he gained far more than he lost.

The knowledge of Christ (v. 8). This means much more than knowledge *about* Christ, because Paul had that kind of historical information before he was saved. To "know Christ" means to have a personal relationship with Him through faith. It is this experience that Jesus mentioned in John 17:3. You and I know *about* many people, even people who lived centuries ago, but we know personally very few. "Christianity *is* Christ." Salvation is know-ing Him in a personal way.

The righteousness of Christ (v. 9). Righteousness was the great goal of Paul's life when he was a Pharisee, but it was a self-righteousness, a works righteousness, that he never really could attain. But when Paul trusted Christ, he lost his own self-righteousness and gained the righteousness of Christ. The technical word for this transaction is *imputation* (read Rom. 4:1–8 carefully). It means "to put to one's account." Paul looked at his own record and discovered that he was spiritually bankrupt. He looked at Christ's record and saw that He was perfect. When Paul trusted Christ, he saw God put Christ's righteousness *to his own account.* More than that, Paul discov-ered that his sins had been put on Christ's account on the cross (2 Cor. 5:21). And God promised Paul that He would never write his sins against him anymore. What a fantastic experience of God's grace!

Romans 9:30—10:13 is a parallel passage, and you ought to read it care-fully. What Paul said about the nation Israel was true in his own life before he was saved. And it is true in the lives of many religious people today; they refuse to abandon their own righteousness that they might receive the free gift of the righteousness of Christ. Many religious people will not even admit they *need* any righteousness. Like Saul of Tarsus, they are measuring them-selves by themselves, or by the standards of the Ten Commandments, and they fail to see the *inwardness* of sin. Paul had to give up his religion to receive righteousness, but he did not consider it a sacrifice.

The fellowship of Christ (vv. 10–11). When he became a Christian, it was not the *end* for Paul, but the *beginning.* His experience with Christ was so tremendous that it transformed his life. And this experience continued in the years to follow. It was a *personal* experience ("That I may know him") as Paul walked with Christ, prayed, obeyed His will, and sought to glorify His name. When he was living under law, all Paul had was a set of rules. But now he had a Friend, a Master, a constant Companion. It was also a *powerful* experience ("and the power of his resurrection"), as the resurrection power of Christ went to work in Paul's life. "Christ liveth in me" (Gal. 2:20). Read Ephesians 1:15–23 and 3:13–21 for Paul's estimate of the resurrection power of Christ and what it can do in your life.

It was also a *painful* experience ("and the fellowship of his sufferings"). Paul knew that it was a privilege to suffer for Christ (Phil. 1:29–30). In fact, suffering had been a part of his experience from the very beginning (Acts 9:16). As we grow in our knowledge of Christ and our experience of His power, we come under the attack of the Enemy. Paul had been a persecutor at one time, but he learned what it means to be persecuted. But it was worth it! For walking with Christ was also a *practical* experience ("being made conformable unto his death"). Paul lived for Christ because he died to self (Rom. 6 explains this); he took up his cross daily and followed Him. The result of this death was a spiritual resurrection (Phil. 3:11) that caused Paul to walk "in newness of life" (Rom. 6:4). Paul summarized this whole experience in Galatians 2:20, so take time to read it.

Yes, Paul gained far more than he lost. In fact, the gains were so thrilling that Paul considered all other "things" nothing but garbage in comparison! No wonder he had joy—his life did not depend on the cheap things of the world but on the eternal values found in Christ. Paul had the "spiritual mind" and looked at the things of earth from heaven's point of view. People who live for things are never really happy, because they must constantly protect their treasures and worry lest they lose their value. Not so the believer with the spiritual mind; his treasures in Christ can never be stolen and they never lose their value.

Maybe now is a good time for you to become an accountant and evaluate in your life the "things" that matter most to you.

QUESTIONS FOR PERSONAL REFLECTION
OR GROUP DISCUSSION

1. What are some of the things (tangibles and intangibles) that may snare us and cause us to lose our Christian joy?

2. What is the basic difference between works righteousness and faith righteousness?

3. Paul described true Christians as ones who boast in Jesus Christ. What does that mean and how do such people differ from merely religious people?

4. Why does the true Christian not put confidence in the flesh?

5. What is the only "good work" that takes the sinner to heaven?

6. Why is sincerity not enough for salvation? How is Paul a good example of this?

7. How was Paul using the wrong measuring stick before he met Jesus? How are people today still doing this?

8. "He is no fool to give what he cannot keep to gain that which he cannot lose." What does that mean to you?

9. Why is the first step to salvation to admit that you need to be saved?

10. Why can't things make us truly happy?

Chapter Nine

LET'S WIN THE RACE!

(Philippians 3:12–16)

Most people read biographies to satisfy their curiosity about great people, hoping also that they may discover the "secret" that made them great. I recall sitting in a grade school assembly program many years ago, listening to an aged doctor who promised to tell us the secret of his long, healthy life. (At one time he was a physician to the president of the United States. I've forgotten which one, but at that stage in my life, it seemed it must have been Washington or Jefferson.) All of us sat there with great expectation, hoping to learn the secret of a long life. At the climax of his address, the doctor told us, "Drink eight glasses of water a day!"

In Philippians 3, Paul gave us his spiritual biography: his past (Phil. 3:1–11), his present (Phil. 3:12–16), and his future (Phil. 3:17–21). We have already met Paul "the accountant," who discovered new values when he met Jesus Christ. In this section we meet Paul "the athlete" with his spiritual vigor, pressing toward the finish line in the Christian race. In the final section we will see Paul "the alien," having his citizenship in heaven and looking for the coming of Jesus Christ. In each of these experiences, Paul was exercising the *spiritual mind;* he was looking at things on earth from

God's point of view. As a result, he was not upset by things behind him, around him, or before him—*things* did not rob him of his joy!

In his letters, Paul used many illustrations from the world to communicate truth about the Christian life. Four are prominent: the military ("Put on the whole armor of God"), architecture ("You are the temple of God"), agriculture ("Whatsoever a man sows, that shall he also reap"), and athletics. In this paragraph, it is Paul the athlete. Bible students are not agreed as to the exact sport Paul was describing, whether the footrace or the chariot race. Either one will do, but my own preference is the chariot race. The Greek chariot, used in the Olympic Games and other events, was really only a small platform with a wheel on each side. The driver had very little to hold on to as he raced around the course. He had to lean forward and strain every nerve and muscle to maintain balance and control the horses. The verb "reaching forth" in Philippians 3:13 literally means "stretching as in a race."

It is important to note that Paul was not telling us how to be saved. If he were, it would be a picture of salvation by works or self-effort, and this would contradict what he wrote in the first eleven verses of Philippians 3. In order to participate in the Greek games, the athlete had to be a citizen. He did not run the race to gain his citizenship. In Philippians 3:20, Paul reminded us that "our conversation [citizenship] is in heaven." Because we are already the children of God through faith in Christ, we have the responsibility of running the race and achieving the goals God has set for us. This is a graphic picture of Philippians 2:12–13: "Work out your own salvation … for it is God which worketh in you." Each believer is on the track; each has a special lane in which to run; and each has a goal to achieve. If we reach the goal the way God has planned, then we receive a reward. If we fail, we lose the reward, but we do not lose our citizenship. (Read 1 Cor. 3:11–15 for the same idea, only using architecture as the symbol.)

All of us want to be "winning Christians" and fulfill the purposes for which we have been saved. What are the essentials for winning the race and one day receiving the reward that is promised?

DISSATISFACTION (3:12–13A)

"Not as though I had already attained." This is the statement of a great Christian who never permitted himself to be satisfied with his spiritual attainments. Obviously, Paul was satisfied with Jesus Christ (Phil. 3:10), but he was not satisfied with his Christian life. A sanctified dissatisfaction is the first essential to progress in the Christian race.

Harry came out of the manager's office with a look on his face dismal enough to wilt the roses on the secretary's desk.

"You didn't get fired?" she asked.

"No, it's not that bad. But he sure did lay into me about my sales record. I can't figure it out; for the past month I've been bringing in plenty of orders. I thought he'd compliment me, but instead he told me to get with it."

Later in the day, the secretary talked to her boss about Harry. The boss chuckled. "Harry is one of our best salesmen, and I'd hate to lose him. But he has a tendency to rest on his laurels and be satisfied with his performance. If I didn't get him mad at me once a month, he'd never produce!"

Many Christians are self-satisfied because they compare their "running" with that of other Christians, usually those who are not making much progress. Had Paul compared himself with others, he would have been tempted to be proud and perhaps to let up a bit. After all, there were not too many believers in Paul's day who had experienced all that he had! But Paul did not compare himself with others; he compared himself with *himself* and with *Jesus Christ*. The dual use of the word *perfect* in Philippians 3:12 and 15 explains his thinking. He has not arrived yet at perfection (Phil. 3:12), but he is "perfect" [mature] (Phil. 3:15), and one mark of this maturity is the knowledge that he is *not* perfect! The mature Christian honestly evaluates himself and strives to do better.

Often in the Bible we are warned against a false estimate of our spiritual condition. The church at Sardis had "a name that thou livest, and art dead" (Rev. 3:1). They had reputation without reality. The church at Laodicea boasted that it was rich, when in God's sight it was "wretched, and miserable, and poor, and blind, and naked" (Rev. 3:17). In contrast to the Laodicean church, the believers at Smyrna thought they were poor when they were really rich (Rev. 2:9). Samson thought he still had his old power, but in reality it had departed from him (Judg. 16:20).

Self-evaluation can be a dangerous thing, because we can err in two directions: (1) making ourselves *better* than we are, or (2) making ourselves *worse* than we really are. Paul had no illusions about himself; he still had to keep "pressing forward" in order to "lay hold of that for which Christ laid hold" of him. A divine dissatisfaction is essential for spiritual progress. "As the hart panteth after the water brooks, so panteth my soul after thee, O God. My soul thirsteth for God, for the living God" (Ps. 42:1–2).

DEVOTION (3:13B)

"One thing" is a phrase that is important to the Christian life. "One thing thou lackest," said Jesus to the self-righteous rich young ruler (Mark 10:21). "One thing is needful," He explained to busy Martha when she criticized her sister (Luke 10:42). "One thing I know," exclaimed the man who had received his sight by the power of Christ (John 9:25). "One thing have I desired of the LORD, that will I seek after," testified the psalmist (Ps. 27:4). Too many Christians are too involved in "*many* things," when the secret of progress is to concentrate on "one thing." It was this decision that was a turning point in D. L. Moody's life. Before the tragedy of the Chicago fire in 1871, Mr. Moody was involved in Sunday school promotion, YMCA work, evangelistic meetings, and many other activities, but after the fire, he determined to devote himself exclusively to evangelism. "This one thing I do" became a reality to him. As a result, millions of people heard the gospel.

The believer must devote himself to running the Christian race. No athlete succeeds by doing everything; he succeeds by *specializing*. There are those few athletes who seem proficient in many sports, but they are the exception. The winners are those who concentrate, who keep their eyes on the goal and let nothing distract them. They are devoted entirely to their calling. Like Nehemiah, the wall-building governor, they reply to the distracting invitations, "I am doing a great work, so that I cannot come down" (Neh. 6:3). "A double minded man is unstable in all his ways" (James 1:8). Concentration is the secret of power. If a river is allowed to overflow its banks, the area around it becomes a swamp. But if that river is dammed and controlled, it becomes a source of power. It is wholly a matter of values and priorities, living for that which matters most.

DIRECTION (3:13C)

The unsaved person is controlled by the past, but the Christian running the race looks toward the future. Imagine what would happen on the race course if the charioteers (or the runners) started looking behind them. It is bad enough for a plowman to look back (Luke 9:62), but for a charioteer to do so means a possible collision and serious injury.

We are accustomed to saying "past, present, future," but we should view time as flowing from the *future* into the *present* and then into the *past*. At least, the believer should be future-oriented, "forgetting those things which are behind." Please keep in mind that in Bible terminology, "to forget" does not mean "to fail to remember." Apart from senility, hypnosis, or a brain malfunction, no mature person can forget what has happened in the past. We may wish that we could erase certain bad memories, but we cannot.

"To forget" in the Bible means "no longer to be influenced by or affected by." When God promises, "Their sins and iniquities will I remember no more" (Heb. 10:17), He is not suggesting that He will conveniently have a bad memory! This is impossible with God. What God is saying is, "I will no longer hold their sins against them. Their sins can no longer affect their standing with Me or influence My attitude toward them."

So, "forgetting those things which are behind" does not suggest an impossible feat of mental and psychological gymnastics by which we try to erase the sins and mistakes of the past. *It simply means that we break the power of the past by living for the future.* We cannot change the past, but we can change the *meaning* of the past. There were things in Paul's past that could have been weights to hold him back (1 Tim. 1:12–17), but they became inspirations to speed him ahead. The events did not change, but his understanding of them changed.

A good example of this principle is Joseph (Gen. 45:1–15). When he met his brothers the second time and revealed himself to them, he held no grudge against them. To be sure, they had mistreated him, but he saw the past from God's point of view. As a result he was unable to hold anything against his brothers. Joseph knew that God had a plan for his life—a race for him to run—and in fulfilling that plan and looking ahead, he broke the power of the past.

Too many Christians are shackled by regrets of the past. They are trying to run the race by looking backward. No wonder they stumble and fall and get in the way of other Christians. Some Christian runners are being distracted by the *successes* of the past, not the failures, and this is just as bad. "The things which are behind" must be set aside and "the things which are before" must take their place.

It is possible to have dissatisfaction, devotion, and direction and still lose the race and the reward. There is a fourth essential.

DETERMINATION (3:14)

"I press." This same verb is translated "I follow after" in Philippians 3:12, and it carries the idea of intense endeavor. The Greeks used it to describe a hunter eagerly pursuing his prey. A man does not become a winning athlete by listening to lectures, watching movies, reading books, or cheering at the games. He becomes a winning athlete by getting into the game and determining to win! The same zeal that Paul employed when he persecuted the church (Phil. 3:6), he displayed in serving Christ. Come to think of it, wouldn't it be wonderful if Christians put as much determination into their spiritual life as they do their golfing, fishing, or bowling?

There are two extremes to avoid here: (1) "*I* must do it all" and (2) "*God* must do it all!" The first describes the activist, the second the quietist, and both are heading for failure. "Let go and let God!" is a clever slogan, but it does not fully describe the process of Christian living. What quarterback would say to his team, "OK, men, just let go and let the coach do it all!" On the other hand, no quarterback would say, "Listen to me and forget what the coach says!" Both extremes are wrong.

The Christian runner with the spiritual mind realizes that God must work *in* him if he is going to win the race (Phil. 2:12–13). "Without me ye can do nothing" (John 15:5). God works *in* us that He might work *through* us. As we apply ourselves to the things of the spiritual life, God is able to mature us and strengthen us for the race. "Exercise thyself rather unto godliness" (1 Tim. 4:7–8). Some Christians are so busy "dying to self" that they never come back to life again to run the race. And others are so sure they can make it on their own that they never stop to read the Word, pray, or ask for the power of the Lord.

Toward what goal is the runner pressing with such spiritual determination? "The prize of the high [upward] calling of God in Christ Jesus" (Phil. 3:14). When he reaches the goal he will receive the reward. Again,

Paul was not suggesting that we attain to heaven by our own efforts. He was simply saying that just as the athlete is rewarded for his performance, so the faithful believer will be crowned when Jesus Christ returns. (See 1 Cor. 9:24–27 for a parallel, and note that while only *one* athlete may receive a prize, *all* Christians may receive the reward. Furthermore, the laurel wreath of the Olympic Games will fade, but the crown Christ gives will never fade.) The important thing is that we reach the goal He has established for us. No matter how successful we may be in the eyes of men, we cannot be rewarded unless we "take hold of that for which Christ Jesus took hold of [us]" (Phil. 3:12 NIV).

DISCIPLINE (3:15–16)

It is not enough to run hard and win the race; the runner must also obey the rules. In the Greek games, the judges were very strict about this. Any infringement of the rules disqualified the athlete. He did not lose his citizenship (though he disgraced it), but he did lose his privilege to participate and win a prize. In Philippians 3:15–16, Paul emphasized the importance of the Christian remembering the spiritual rules laid down in the Word.

One of the greatest athletes ever to come out of the United States was Jim Thorpe. At the 1912 Olympics at Stockholm, he won the pentathlon and the decathlon, and was undoubtedly the hero of the games. But the next year officials found that Thorpe had played semiprofessional baseball and therefore had forfeited his amateur standing. This meant that he had to return his gold medals and his trophy, and that his Olympic achievements were erased from the records. It was a high price to pay for breaking the rules. (Thorpe's medals were reinstated in 1985 by the Olympic Committee.)

This was what Paul had in mind in 1 Corinthians 9:24–27. "Any man who enters an athletic contest practices rigid self-control in training"

(Phil. 3:25 wms). If the athlete breaks training, he is disqualified; if he breaks the rules of the game, he is disqualified. "No contestant in the games is crowned, unless he competes according to the rules" (2 Tim. 2:5 wms). The issue is not what *he* thinks or what the *spectators* think but what the judges say. One day each Christian will stand before the judgment seat of Christ (Rom. 14:10–12). The Greek word for "judgment seat" is *bema,* the very same word used to describe the place where the Olympic judges gave out the prizes. If we have disciplined ourselves to obey the rules, we shall receive a prize.

Bible history is filled with people who began the race with great success but failed at the end because they disregarded God's rules. They did not lose their salvation, but they did lose their rewards (1 Cor. 3:15). It happened to Lot (Gen. 19), Samson (Judg. 16), Saul (1 Sam. 28; 31), and Ananias and Sapphira (Acts 5). And it can happen to us. It is an exciting experience to run the race daily, "looking unto Jesus" (Heb. 12:2). It will be even more exciting when we experience that "upward calling" and Jesus returns to take us to heaven. Then we will stand before the *bema* to receive our rewards. It was this future prospect that motivated Paul, and it can also motivate us.

QUESTIONS FOR PERSONAL REFLECTION OR GROUP DISCUSSION

1. Why did things behind, around, and before Paul not upset him or rob him of his joy?

2. Why is a "sanctified dissatisfaction" essential in the Christian race?

3. What happens when Christians compare their "running" with that of other Christians?

4. How can self-evaluation be a dangerous thing?

5. Why is it important for each believer to be devoted to his or her specific calling? Where can you improve on this?

6. What does the author mean when he says we need to "break the power of the past by living for the future"?

7. Do you think most Christians today put as much determination into their Christian race as they do into their jobs? Their leisure activities? Explain.

8. Why is it necessary for the Christian runner to obey the rules of the race?

9. How do we discover the rules for our Christian race?

Chapter Ten

LIVING IN THE FUTURE TENSE

(Philippians 3:17–21)

How strange in a letter filled with joy to find Paul *weeping*. Perhaps he was weeping over himself and his difficult situation. No, he was a man with a *single mind,* and his circumstances did not discourage him. Was he weeping because of what some of the Roman Christians were doing to him? No, he had the *submissive mind* and would not permit people to rob him of his joy. These tears were not for himself at all; they were shed because of others. Because Paul had the *spiritual mind,* he was heartbroken over the way some professed Christians were living, people who "mind earthly things."

While we cannot be sure, it is likely that Philippians 3:18–19 describes the Judaizers and their followers. Certainly Paul was writing about professed Christians and not people outside the church. The Judaizers were the "enemies of the cross of Christ" in that they added the law of Moses to the work of redemption that Christ wrought on the cross. Their obedience to the Old Testament dietary laws would make a god out of the belly (see Col. 2:20–23), and their emphasis on circumcision would amount to glorying in that about which they ought to be ashamed (see Gal. 6:12–15). These men were not spiritually minded; they were earthly minded. They were holding on to earthly rituals and beliefs that God had given to Israel, and they were opposing the heavenly blessings that the Christian has in Christ (Eph. 1:3; 2:6; Col. 3:1–3).

The word *spiritual* has suffered as much abuse as the word *fellowship*. Too many people think that a "spiritual Christian" is mystical, dreamy, impractical, and distant. When he prays, he shifts his voice into a sepulchral tone *in tremolo* and goes to great lengths to inform God of the things He already knows. Unfortunately, this kind of unctuous piety is a poor example of true spirituality. To be spiritually minded does not require one to be impractical and mystical. Quite the contrary, the spiritual mind makes the believer think more clearly and get things done more efficiently.

To be "spiritually minded" simply means to look at earth from heaven's point of view. "Give your heart to the heavenly things, not to the passing things of earth" (Col. 3:2 PH). "Practice occupying your minds with the things above, not with the things on earth" (Col. 3:2 WMS). D. L. Moody used to scold Christians for being "so heavenly minded they were no earthly good," and that exhortation still needs to be heeded. Christians have a dual citizenship—on earth and in heaven—and our citizenship in heaven ought to make us better people here on earth. The spiritually minded believer is not attracted by the things of this world. He makes his decisions on the basis of eternal values and not the passing fads of society. Lot chose the well-watered plain of Jordan because his values were worldly, and ultimately he lost everything. Moses refused the pleasures and treasures of Egypt because he had something infinitely more wonderful to live for (Heb. 11:24–26). "What shall it profit a man, if he shall gain the whole world, and lose his own soul?" (Mark 8:36).

"For our citizenship is in heaven" (Phil. 3:20 NASB). The Greek word translated "conversation" or "citizenship" is the word from which we get the English word *politics*. It has to do with one's behavior as a citizen of a nation. Paul was encouraging us to have the spiritual mind, and he did this by pointing out the characteristics of the Christian whose citizenship is in heaven. Just as Philippi was a colony of Rome on foreign soil, so the church is a "colony of heaven" on earth.

OUR NAMES ARE ON HEAVEN'S RECORD

The citizens of Philippi were privileged to be Roman citizens away from Rome. When a baby was born in Philippi, it was important that its name be registered on the legal records. When the lost sinner trusts Christ and becomes a citizen of heaven, his name is written in "the book of life" (Phil. 4:3).

Citizenship is important. When you travel to another country, it is essential that you have a passport that proves your citizenship. None of us wants to suffer the fate of Philip Nolan in the classic tale *The Man Without a Country.* Because he cursed the name of his country, Nolan was sentenced to live aboard ship and never again see his native land or even hear its name or news about its progress. For fifty-six years he was on an endless journey from ship to ship and sea to sea and finally was buried at sea. He was a "man without a country."

The Christian's name is written in "the book of life," and this is what determines his final entrance into the heavenly country (Rev. 20:15). When you confess Christ on earth, He confesses your name in heaven (Matt. 10:32–33). Your name is written down in heaven (Luke 10:20), and it stands written forever. (The Greek verb "written" in Luke 10:20 is in the perfect tense: "it is once-for-all written and stands written.")

A friend in Washington, D.C., arranged for my oldest son and me to tour the White House. She told us to be at a certain gate at eight o'clock in the morning and to be prepared to show evidence of who we were. David and I walked up to the gate, and the guard politely asked our names. We told him, showing our credentials. He said, "Yes, sir! Mr. Warren Wiersbe and David! You may enter!" We got into the White House because our names were written down on the proper list, and our names got on that list through the intercession of another. So it is with our entrance into heaven: Because we have trusted Christ, our names are written down, and we will enter glory on His merits and intercession alone.

WE SPEAK HEAVEN'S LANGUAGE

Those who "mind earthly things" *talk* about earthly things. After all, what comes out of the mouth reveals what is in the heart (Matt. 12:34–37). The unsaved person does not understand the things of God's Spirit (1 Cor. 2:14–16), so how can he talk about them intelligently? The citizens of heaven understand spiritual things and enjoy discussing them and sharing them with one another.

"They are of the world: therefore speak they of the world, and the world heareth them. We are of God: he that knoweth God heareth us; he that is not of God heareth not us. Hereby know we the spirit of truth, and the spirit of error" (1 John 4:5–6).

But speaking heaven's language not only involves what we say, but also the way we say it. The spiritually minded Christian doesn't go around quoting Bible verses all day! But he is careful to speak in a manner that glorifies God. "Let your speech be always with grace, seasoned with salt, that ye may know how ye ought to answer every man" (Col. 4:6). No believer ought ever to say, "Now take this with a grain of salt!" *Put the salt into your speech!* Salt prevents corruption. "Let no corrupt communication proceed out of your mouth, but that which is good to the use of edifying, that it may minister grace unto the hearers" (Eph. 4:29).

WE OBEY HEAVEN'S LAWS

The citizens of Philippi were governed by Roman law, not Greek law, even though they were located hundreds of miles away from Rome. In fact, it was this policy that put Paul into jail when he first visited Philippi (Acts 16:16–24). Paul himself used his Roman citizenship to guarantee his protection under Roman law (Acts 16:35–40; 21:33–40; 22:24–30).

In Philippians 3:17, Paul warned the Philippian believers against imitating the wrong kind of citizens. "Be followers together of me." Of course, Paul was a follower of Christ, so his admonition is not egotistical! (1 Cor. 11:1). Paul knew himself to be an "alien" in this world, a "pilgrim and a stranger" (see 1 Peter 2:11). His life was governed by heaven's laws, and this is what made him different. He was concerned about others, not himself. He was interested in giving, not getting. His motive was love (2 Cor. 5:14), not hatred. By faith, Paul obeyed the Word of God, knowing that one day he would be rewarded. Men might oppose him and persecute him now, but in that final day of reckoning, he would be the winner.

Sad to say, there are those today, like the Judaizers in Paul's day, who profess to be citizens of heaven, but whose lives do not show it. They may be zealous in their religious activities and even austere in their disciplines, but there is no evidence of the control of the Spirit of God in their lives. All that they do is energized by the flesh, and they get all the glory. It is bad enough that they are going astray, but they also lead other people astray. No wonder Paul wept over them.

He Is Loyal to Heaven's Cause

The cross of Jesus Christ is the theme of the Bible, the heart of the gospel, and the chief source of praise in heaven (Rev. 5:8–10). The cross is the proof of God's love for sinners (Rom. 5:8) and God's hatred for sin. The cross condemns what the world values. It judges mankind and pronounces the true verdict: *Guilty!*

In what sense were the Judaizers the "enemies of the cross of Christ"? For one thing, the cross ended the Old Testament religion. When the veil of the temple was torn in two, God was announcing that the way to God was open through Christ (Heb. 10:19–25). When Jesus said, "It is finished," He made one sacrifice for sins, and thus ended the whole sacrificial system (Heb. 10:1–14). By His death and resurrection, Jesus accomplished a "spiritual circumcision" that made ritual circumcision unnecessary (Col. 2:10–13). Everything that the Judaizers advocated had been eliminated by the death of Christ on the cross.

Furthermore, everything that they lived for was condemned by the cross. Jesus had broken down the wall that stood between Jews and Gentiles (Eph. 2:14–16), and the Judaizers were rebuilding that wall! They were obeying "carnal [fleshly] ordinances" (Heb. 9:10), regulations that appealed to the flesh and were not directed by the Spirit. But the true believer crucifies the flesh (Gal. 5:24). He also crucifies the world (Gal. 6:14). Yet the Judaizers were minding "earthly things." It is the cross that is central in the life of the believer. He does not glory in men, in religion, or in his own achievements; he glories in the cross (Gal. 6:14).

Paul wept because he knew the future of these men: "whose end is destruction" (Phil. 3:19). This word carries with it the idea of waste and "lostness." (It is translated "waste" in Mark 14:4.) Judas is called "the son of perdition," and this is the word used (John 17:12). A wasted life and an eternity of waste! In contrast, the true child of God, whose citizenship is in heaven, has a bright future.

WE ARE LOOKING FOR HEAVEN'S LORD

The Judaizers were living in the past tense, trying to get the Philippian believers to go back to Moses and the law, but true Christians live in the future tense, anticipating the return of their Savior (Phil. 3:20–21). As the *accountant* in Philippians 3:1–11, Paul discovered new *values*. As the *athlete* in Philippians 3:12–16, he displayed new *vigor*. Now as the *alien,* he experiences a new *vision:* "We look for the Saviour." It is this anticipation of the coming of Christ that motivates the believer with the spiritual mind.

There is tremendous energy in the present power of a future hope. Because Abraham looked for a city, he was content to live in a tent (Heb. 11:13–16). Because Moses looked for the rewards of heaven, he was willing to forsake the treasures of earth (Heb. 11:24–26). Because of the "joy that was set before him" (Heb. 12:2), Jesus was willing to endure the cross. The fact that Jesus Christ is returning is a powerful motive for dedicated living and devoted service *today.* "And every man that hath this hope in him purifieth himself, even as he is pure" (read 1 John 2:28—3:3).

The citizen of heaven, living on earth, is never discouraged because he knows that his Lord is one day going to return. He faithfully keeps on doing his job lest his Lord return and find him disobedient (Luke 12:40–48). The spiritually minded believer does not live for the things of this world; he anticipates the blessings of the world to come. This does not mean that he ignores or neglects his daily obligations, but it does mean that what he does today is governed by what Christ will do in the future.

Paul mentioned particularly that the believer will receive a glorified body, like the body of Christ. Today we live in a "body of humiliation" (which is the meaning of the word translated "vile" in Phil. 3:21), but when we see Christ, we will receive a body of glory. It will happen in a moment, in the twinkling of an eye (1 Cor. 15:42–53). At that moment, all the things of this world will be worthless to us—just as they ought to be, relatively, today. If we are living in the future tense, then we will be exercising the spiritual mind and living for the things that really matter.

When Jesus returns, He will "subdue all things unto himself" (Phil. 3:21b). That word *subdue* means "to arrange in ranks." Isn't that our problem today? *We do not arrange things in their proper order.* Our values are twisted. Consequently, our vigor is wasted on useless activities, and our vision is clouded so that the return of Christ is not a real motivating power in our lives. Living in the future tense means letting Christ arrange the things in life according to the proper rank. It means living with eternity's values in view, and daring to believe God's promise that "he that doeth the will of God abideth forever" (1 John 2:17).

QUESTIONS FOR PERSONAL REFLECTION
OR GROUP DISCUSSION

1. What does it mean to be "spiritually minded"? How can you improve this area of your own life?

2. Why is perspective as important as knowledge in being "spiritually minded"?

3. How does a Christian's "dual citizenship" affect his or her life?

4. What does it mean to speak "heaven's language"? Give some practical examples.

5. How are "heaven's laws" for the Christian like a fence around a flock of sheep?

6. How did the cross end the Old Testament religion?

7. "The true believer crucifies the flesh." What does that mean in practical, everyday terms?

8. How is our future hope of Jesus returning a powerful motive for dedicated living and service today?

9. What does the author mean when he says that what the Christian does today is governed by what Christ will do in the future?

10. How are our values twisted today? What effect does that have on our Christian lives?

Chapter Eleven

You Don't Have to Worry!

(Philippians 4:1–9)

I f anybody had an excuse for worrying, it was the apostle Paul. His beloved Christian friends at Philippi were disagreeing with one another, and he was not there to help them. We have no idea what Euodia and Syntyche were disputing about, but whatever it was, it was bringing division into the church. Along with the potential division at Philippi, Paul had to face division among the believers at Rome (Phil. 1:14–17). Added to these burdens was the possibility of his own death! Yes, Paul had a good excuse to worry—*but he did not.* Instead, he took time to explain to us the secret of victory over worry.

What is worry? The Greek word translated "careful" (anxious) in Philippians 4:6 means "to be pulled in different directions." Our hopes pull us in one direction; our fears pull us the opposite direction; and we are pulled apart! The Old English root from which we get our word *worry* means "to strangle." If you have ever really worried, you know how it does strangle a person. In fact, worry has definite physical consequences: headaches, neck pains, ulcers, even back pains. Worry affects our thinking, our digestion, and even our coordination.

From the spiritual point of view, worry is *wrong thinking* (the mind) and *wrong feeling* (the heart) about circumstances, people, and things. Worry is the greatest thief of joy. It is not enough for us, however, to tell ourselves to quit worrying because that will never capture the thief. Worry is an inside job, and it takes more than good intentions to get the victory. The antidote to worry is the *secure mind:* "The peace of God … shall keep [garrison, guard like a soldier] your hearts and minds through Christ Jesus" (Phil. 4:7). When you have the secure mind, the peace of God guards you and the God of peace guides you (Phil. 4:9). With that kind of protection— why worry?

If we are to conquer worry and experience the secure mind, we must meet the conditions that God has laid down. There are three: right praying (Phil. 4:6–7), right thinking (Phil. 4:8), and right living (Phil. 4:9).

1. RIGHT PRAYING (4:6–7)

Paul did not write, "Pray about it!" He was too wise to do that. He used three different words to describe "right praying": *prayer, supplication,* and *thanksgiving.* Right praying involves all three. The word *prayer* is the general word for making requests known to the Lord. It carries the idea of adoration, devotion, and worship. Whenever we find ourselves worrying, our first action ought to be to get alone with God and worship Him. Adoration is what is needed. We must see the greatness and majesty of God! We must realize that He is big enough to solve our problems. Too often we rush into His presence and hastily tell Him our needs, when we ought to approach His throne calmly and in deepest reverence. The first step in right praying is *adoration.*

The second is *supplication,* an earnest sharing of our needs and problems. There is no place for halfhearted, insincere prayer! While we know we are not heard for our "much speaking" (Matt. 6:7–8), still we realize that our Father wants us to be earnest in our asking (Matt. 7:1–11). This is the way Jesus prayed in the garden (Heb. 5:7), and while His closest disciples were sleeping, Jesus was sweating great drops of blood! Supplication is not a matter of carnal energy but of spiritual intensity (Rom. 15:30; Col. 4:12).

After adoration and supplication comes *appreciation,* giving thanks to God (see Eph. 5:20; Col. 3:15–17). Certainly the Father enjoys hearing His children say, "Thank You!" When Jesus healed ten lepers, only one of the ten returned to give thanks (Luke 17:11–19), and we wonder if the percentage is any higher today. We are eager to ask but slow to appreciate.

You will note that right praying is not something every Christian can do immediately, because right praying depends on the right kind of mind. This is why Paul's formula for peace is found at the *end* of Philippians and not at the *beginning.* If we have the *single mind* of Philippians 1 then we can give *adoration.* (How can a double-minded person ever praise God?) If we have the *submissive mind* of Philippians 2, we can come with *supplication.* (Would a person with a proud mind ask God for something?) If we have the *spiritual mind* of Philippians 3 we can show our *appreciation.* (A worldly minded person would not know that God had given him anything to appreciate!) In other words, we must practice Philippians 1, 2, and 3 if we are going to experience the *secure mind* of Philippians 4.

Paul counseled us to take everything to God in prayer. "Don't worry about *anything,* but pray about *everything!"* was his admonition (see Phil. 4:6). We are prone to pray about the "big things" in life and forget to pray about the so-called "little things"—until they grow and become big things! Talking to God about *everything* that concerns us and Him is the first step toward victory over worry.

The result is that the "peace of God" guards the heart and the mind. You will remember that Paul was chained to a Roman soldier, guarded day and night. In like manner, the peace of God stands guard over the two areas that create worry—the heart (wrong feeling) and the mind (wrong thinking). When we give our hearts to Christ in salvation, we experience "peace with God" (Rom. 5:1), but the peace of God takes us a step further into His blessings. This does not mean the absence of trials on the outside, but it does mean a quiet confidence within, regardless of circumstances, people, or things.

Daniel gave us a wonderful illustration of peace through prayer. When the king announced that none of his subjects was to pray to anyone except the king, Daniel went to his room, opened his windows, and prayed as before (Dan. 6:1–10). Note how Daniel prayed. He "prayed, and gave thanks before his God" (Dan. 6:10) and he made "supplication" (Dan. 6:11). Prayer—supplication—thanksgiving. And the result was perfect peace *in the midst of difficulty*. Daniel was able to spend the night with the lions in perfect peace, while the king *in his palace* could not sleep (Dan. 6:18).

The first condition for the secure mind and victory over worry is right praying.

2. RIGHT THINKING (4:8)

Peace involves the heart *and the mind*. "Thou wilt keep him in perfect peace, whose mind is stayed on thee: because he trusteth in thee" (Isa. 26:3). Wrong thinking leads to wrong feeling, and before long the heart and mind are pulled apart and we are strangled by worry. We must realize that thoughts are real and powerful, even though they cannot be seen, weighed, or measured. We must bring "into captivity every thought to the obedience of Christ" (2 Cor. 10:5).

Sow a thought, reap an action.

Sow an action, reap a habit.

Sow a habit, reap a character.

Sow a character, reap a destiny!

Paul spells out in detail the things we ought to think about as Christians.

Whatever is true. Dr. Walter Cavert reported a survey on worry that indicated that only 8 percent of the things people worried about were legitimate matters of concern. The other 92 percent either were imaginary, never happened, or involved matters over which the people had no control anyway. Satan is the liar (John 8:44), and he wants to corrupt our minds with his lies (2 Cor. 11:3). "Yea, hath God said …?" is the way he approaches us, just as he approached Eve (Gen. 3:1ff.). The Holy Spirit controls our minds through truth (John 17:17; 1 John 5:6), but the Devil tries to control them through lies. *Whenever we believe a lie, Satan takes over.*

Whatever is honest and just. This means "worthy of respect and right." There are many things that are not respectable, and Christians should not think about these things. This does not mean we hide our heads in the sand and avoid what is unpleasant and displeasing, but it does mean we do not focus our attention on dishonorable things and permit them to control our thoughts.

Whatever is pure, lovely, and of good report. "Pure" probably refers to moral purity, since the people then, as now, were constantly attacked by temptations to sexual impurity (Eph. 4:17–24; 5:8–12). "Lovely" means "beautiful, attractive." "Of good report" means "worth talking about, appealing." The believer must major on the high and noble thoughts, not the base thoughts of this corrupt world.

Whatever possesses virtue and praise. If it has *virtue,* it will motivate us to do better, and if it has *praise,* it is worth commending to others. No Christian can afford to waste mind power on thoughts that tear him down or that would tear others down if these thoughts were shared.

If you will compare this list to David's description of the Word of God in Psalm 19:7–9, you will see a parallel. The Christian who fills his heart and mind with God's Word will have a built-in "radar" for detecting wrong thoughts. "Great peace have they which love thy law" (Ps. 119:165). Right thinking is the result of daily meditation on the Word of God.

3. RIGHT LIVING (4:9)

You cannot separate outward action and inward attitude. Sin always results in unrest (unless the conscience is seared), and purity ought to result in peace. "And the work of righteousness shall be peace; and the effect of righteousness quietness and peace" (Isa. 32:17). "But the wisdom that is from above is first pure, then peaceable" (James 3:17). Right living is a necessary condition for experiencing the peace of God.

Paul balances four activities: "learned, and received" and "heard, and seen." It is one thing to *learn* a truth, but quite another to *receive* it inwardly and make it a part of our inner man (see 1 Thess. 2:13). Facts in the head are not enough; we must also have truths in the heart. In Paul's ministry, he not only *taught* the Word but also *lived* it so that his listeners could see the truth in his life. Paul's experience ought to be our experience. We must learn the Word, receive it, hear it, and do it. "Be ye doers of the word, and not hearers only" (James 1:22).

"The peace of God" is one test of whether or not we are in the will of God. "Let the peace that Christ can give keep on acting as umpire in your hearts" (Col. 3:15 WMS). If we are walking with the Lord, then the peace of God and the God of peace exercise their influence over our hearts. Whenever we disobey, we lose that peace and we know we have done something wrong. God's peace is the "umpire" that calls us "out"!

Right praying, right thinking, and right living: These are the conditions for having the secure mind and victory over worry. As Philippians 4 is the peace chapter of the New Testament, James 4 is the war chapter. It begins with a question: "From whence come wars and fightings among you?" James explained the causes of war: *wrong praying* ("Ye ask, and receive not, because ye ask amiss," James 4:3), *wrong thinking* ("purify your hearts, ye double minded," James 4:8), and *wrong living* ("know ye not that the friendship of the world is enmity with God?" James 4:4). There is no middle ground. Either we yield heart and mind to the Spirit of God and practice right praying, thinking, and living; or we yield to the flesh and find ourselves torn apart by worry.

There is no need to worry! And worry is a sin! (Have you read Matt. 6:24–34 lately?) With the peace of God to guard us and the God of peace to guide us—*why worry?*

QUESTIONS FOR PERSONAL REFLECTION
OR GROUP DISCUSSION

1. What is worry?

2. What kinds of things do you worry about? Has worry ever accomplished anything good for you?

3. What is the antidote to worry?

4. What are the three conditions we must meet to conquer worry?

5. When we find ourselves worrying, what should our first action be? Why?

6. What is supplication?

7. How can we have peace and not worry in the midst of difficulty?

8. How can we focus on what is "pure," "lovely," and "of good report" while in a world of immorality and corruption?

9. How can we have a built-in "radar" for detecting wrong thoughts?

10. How is the peace of God a test of whether we're in the will of God?

Chapter Twelve

THE SECRET OF CONTENTMENT

(Philippians 4:10–23)

The trouble with him is that he's a thermometer and not a thermostat!" This statement by one of his deacons aroused the pastor's curiosity. They were discussing possible board members, and Jim's name had come up.

"Pastor, it's like this," the deacon explained. "A thermometer doesn't change anything around it—it just registers the temperature. It's always going up and down. But a thermostat regulates the surroundings and changes them when they need to be changed. Jim is a thermometer—he lacks the power to change things. Instead, they change him!"

The apostle Paul was a thermostat. Instead of having spiritual ups and downs as the situation changed, he went right on, steadily doing his work and serving Christ. His personal references at the close of this letter indicate that he was not the victim of circumstances but the victor over circumstances: I can accept all things (Phil. 4:11); "I can do all things" (Phil. 4:13); I have all things (Phil. 4:18). Paul did not have to be pampered to be content; he found his contentment in the spiritual resources abundantly provided by Christ.

Contentment is not complacency, nor is it a false peace based on ignorance. The complacent believer is unconcerned about others, while the contented Christian wants to share his blessings. Contentment is not escape from the battle, but rather an abiding peace and confidence in the midst of the battle. "I have learned, in whatsoever state I am, therewith to be content" (Phil. 4:11). Two words in that verse are vitally important—"learned" and "content."

The verb *learned* means "learned by experience." Paul's spiritual contentment was not something he had immediately after he was saved. He had to go through many difficult experiences of life in order to learn how to be content. The word *content* actually means "contained." It is a description of the man whose resources are within him so that he does not have to depend on substitutes without. The Greek word means "self-sufficient" and was a favorite word of the stoic philosophers. But the Christian is not sufficient in himself; he is sufficient in Christ. Because Christ lives within us, we are adequate for the demands of life.

In this chapter, Paul named three wonderful spiritual resources that make us adequate and give us contentment.

1. THE OVERRULING PROVIDENCE OF GOD (4:10)

In this day of scientific achievement, we hear less and less about the providence of God. We sometimes get the idea that the world is a vast natural machine and that even God Himself cannot interrupt the wheels as they are turning. But the Word of God clearly teaches the providential workings of God in nature and in the lives of His people. The word *providence* comes from two Latin words: *pro,* meaning "before," and *video,* meaning "to see." God's providence simply means that God sees to it beforehand. It does not mean that God simply *knows* beforehand, because providence involves much more. It is the working of God in advance to arrange circumstances and situations for the fulfilling of His purposes.

The familiar story of Joseph and his brothers illustrates the meaning of providence (Gen. 37—50). Joseph's brothers envied him and sold him as a slave when he was only seventeen years old. He was taken to Egypt, and there God revealed that seven years of famine were coming after seven years of plenty. It was through Joseph's interpretation of Pharaoh's dreams that this fact was discovered. Because of that, Joseph was elevated to the position of second ruler in Egypt. After twenty years of separation, Joseph's brothers were reconciled to him, and they understood what the Lord had done.

"God did send me before you to preserve life," Joseph said (Gen. 45:5). "But as for you, ye thought evil against me; but God meant it unto good" (Gen. 50:20). This is the providence of God: His hand ruling and overruling in the affairs of life. Paul experienced this divine providence in his life and ministry, and he was able to write, "We know that all things work together for good to them that love God, to them that are the called according to his purpose" (Rom. 8:28). God in His providence had caused the church at Philippi to become concerned about Paul's needs, and it came at the very time Paul needed their love most! They had been concerned, but they had lacked the opportunity to help. Many Christians today have the opportunities, but they lack the concern!

Life is not a series of accidents; it is a series of appointments. "I will guide thee with mine eye" (Ps. 32:8). Abraham called God "Jehovah-Jireh," meaning "the Lord will see to it" (Gen. 22:14). "When he putteth forth his own sheep, he goeth before them" (John 10:4). This is the providence of God, a wonderful source of contentment.

2. THE UNFAILING POWER OF GOD (4:11–13)

Paul was quick to let his friends know that he was not complaining. His happiness did not depend on circumstances or things; his joy came from something deeper, something apart from either poverty or prosperity. Most of us have learned how to "be abased," because when difficulties come we immediately run to the Lord. But few have learned how "to abound." Prosperity has done more damage to believers than has adversity. "I am rich, and increased with goods, and have need of nothing" (Rev. 3:17).

The word *instructed* in Philippians 4:12 is not the same as "learned" in Philippians 4:11. "Instructed" means "initiated into the secret." This word was used by the pagan religions with reference to their "inner secrets." Through trial and testing, Paul was initiated into the wonderful secret of contentment in spite of poverty or prosperity. "I can do all things through Christ which strengtheneth me" (Phil. 4:13). It was the power of Christ within him that gave him spiritual contentment.

Fog had moved into O'Hare Field, the airport that serves Chicago, and my departure had been delayed. I was sitting in the terminal reading a book and quietly asking God to work out His plans for the trip. Near me was a gentleman waiting for the same plane, but he was pacing up and down like a caged lion, and the language he was using to describe the fog was making the atmosphere more dense! I thought, *Here is a man without any inner resources.* Later, he asked me how I could be so calm when the planes were all late, and I had the opportunity to share the gospel with him.

While flying back to Chicago from upper New York via New York City, we had to stay in our holding pattern over Kennedy Airport for more than an hour. When the flight attendant announced that we would be landing an hour late, a man across the aisle shouted, "Bring out the booze!" This was his only resource when things were going against him.

All of nature depends on hidden resources. The great trees send their roots down into the earth to draw up water and minerals. Rivers have their sources in the snow-capped mountains. The most important part of a tree is the part you cannot see, the root system, and the most important part of the Christian's life is the part that only God sees. Unless we draw on the deep resources of God by faith, we fail against the pressures of life. Paul depended on the power of Christ at work in his life (see Phil. 1:6, 21; 2:12–13; 3:10). "I can—through Christ" was Paul's motto, and it can be our motto too.

"I am ready for anything through the strength of the One who lives within me," is the way J. B. Phillips translated Philippians 4:13. The Living Bible puts it this way: "I can do everything God asks me to with the help of Christ who gives me the strength and power." No matter which translation you prefer, they all say the same thing: the Christian has all the power *within* that he needs to be adequate for the demands of life. We need only release this power by faith.

Every Christian ought to read *Hudson Taylor's Spiritual Secret* by Dr. and Mrs. Howard Taylor, because it illustrates this principle of inner power in the life of a great missionary to China. For many years, Hudson Taylor worked hard and felt that he was trusting Christ to meet his needs, but somehow he had no joy or liberty in his ministry. Then a letter from a friend opened his eyes to the adequacy of Christ. "It is not by trusting my own faithfulness, but by looking away to the Faithful One!" he said. This was a turning point in his life. Moment by moment, he drew on the power of Christ for every responsibility of the day, and Christ's power carried him through.

Jesus taught this same lesson in the sermon on the vine and branches in John 15. He is the Vine; we are the branches. A branch is good only for bearing fruit; otherwise you may as well burn it. The branch does not bear fruit through its own self-effort, but by drawing on the life of the Vine. "Without me, ye can do nothing" (John 15:5). As the believer maintains his communion with Christ, the power of God is there to see him through. "I am self-sufficient in Christ's sufficiency" (Phil. 4:13 AB).

The overruling providence of God and the unfailing power of God are two spiritual resources on which we can draw that we might be adequate for the tasks of life. But there is a third resource.

3. THE UNCHANGING PROMISE OF GOD (4:10–20)

Paul thanked the church at Philippi for their generous gift. He compared their giving to three very familiar things.

(1) A budding tree (v. 10). The word *flourished* carries the idea of a flower or tree budding or blossoming. Often we go through "winter seasons" spiritually, but then the spring arrives and there is new life and blessing. The tree itself is not picked up and moved; the circumstances are not changed. The difference is *the new life within*.

(2) An investment (vv. 14–17). Paul looked on their missionary gift as an investment that would pay them rich spiritual dividends. The word *communicate* is our familiar word "fellowship." The church entered into an arrangement of giving and receiving; the church gave *materially* to Paul and received *spiritually* from the Lord. The Lord keeps the books and will never fail to pay one spiritual dividend. That church is poor that fails to share materially with others.

(3) A sacrifice (v. 18). Paul looked on their gift as a spiritual sacrifice, laid on the altar to the glory of God. There are such things as "spiritual sacrifices" in the Christian life (see 1 Peter 2:5). We are to yield our bodies as spiritual sacrifices (Rom. 12:1–2), as well as the praise of our lips (Heb. 13:15). Good works are a sacrifice to the Lord (Heb. 13:16), and so are the lost souls that we are privileged to win to Christ (Rom. 15:16). Here, Paul saw the Philippian believers as priests, giving their offering as a sacrifice to the Lord. In the light of Malachi 1:6–14, we need to present the very finest that we have to the Lord.

But Paul did not see this gift as simply coming from Philippi. He saw it as the supply of his need from heaven. Paul's trust was in the Lord. There is an interesting contrast between Philippians 4:18 and 19. We might state it this way if we were to paraphrase Paul: "You met *my* need, and God is going to meet *your* need. You met *one* need that I have, but my God will meet *all* of your needs. You gave out of your *poverty,* but God will supply your needs out of His *riches* in glory."

God has not promised to supply all our *greeds.* When the child of God is in the will of God, serving for the glory of God, then he will have every need met. Hudson Taylor often said, "When God's work is done in God's way for God's glory, it will not lack for God's supply."

A young pastor came to a church that had been accustomed to raising its annual budget by means of suppers, bazaars, and the like. He told his officers he could not agree with their program. "Let's pray and ask God to meet every need," he suggested. "At the end of the month, pay all the bills and leave my salary till the last. If there isn't enough money for my salary, then I'm the one who suffers, and not the church. But I don't think anybody is going to suffer." The officers were sure that both the pastor and the church would die, but such was not the case. Each month every bill was paid, and at the end of the year there was a surplus in the treasury for the first time in many years.

Contentment comes from adequate resources. Our resources are the providence of God, the power of God, and the promises of God. These resources made Paul sufficient for every demand of life, and they can make us sufficient too.

QUESTIONS FOR PERSONAL REFLECTION
OR GROUP DISCUSSION

1. What is contentment? In what areas of your life do you struggle with this? How can you improve in this?

2. What is the difference between being complacent and being content?

3. Is contentment born in us or learned? Explain.

4. What is God's providence?

5. How does Romans 8:28 help us trust in God's providence?

6. Why do you think prosperity has done more damage to believers than adversity?

7. What does the author mean when he says, "The most important part of the Christian's life is the part that only God sees"?

8. If Christians truly believe Philippians 4:13, why aren't we doing more for the Lord?

9. Hudson Taylor said, "When God's work is done in God's way for God's glory, it will not lack for God's supply." Do you agree? Why or why not?

10. How can our contentment be a witness to the lost?

Chapter Thirteen

PUTTING PHILIPPIANS TO WORK

Now that you have completed your study of this exciting and practical letter, *don't lose what you have learned.* The best thing about Bible study isn't the learning but the *living.* So, here are a few suggestions for keeping the joy in your life.

1. Surrender your mind to the Lord at the beginning of each day. This is a part of dedication: "I beseech you therefore, brethren, by the mercies of God, that ye present your *bodies* a living sacrifice.… And be not conformed to this world: but be ye transformed by the renewing of your *mind,* that ye may prove what is that good, and acceptable, and perfect *will* of God" (Rom. 12:1–2). Give God your body, mind, and will—by faith—as you start each day.

2. Let the Holy Spirit renew your mind through the Word. Daily systematic reading of the Bible is a must if you are going to have victory and joy.

3. As you pray, ask God to give you that day a single mind, a submissive mind, a spiritual mind, a secure mind. As you contemplate the day's schedule, be sure that nothing you have planned robs you of the joy God wants you to have. Perhaps you must meet a person you don't especially like. Ask God to give you the submissive mind that you will need. Or maybe you must go through a difficult experience. Then be sure you have the single mind, concerned with Christ and the gospel, and not only with your own personal likes and dislikes.

4. *During the day, "mind your mind."* If you find yourself losing your inner peace and joy, stop and take inventory: *Do I have the single mind? Did I just miss an opportunity to glorify Christ? Or was I a bit pushy, so that I lost the submissive mind?* If you discover you have sinned, then immediately confess it to the Lord (1 John 1:9). If possible, go back and remedy your mistake. If this cannot be done, ask God to give you another opportunity for witness.

5. *Guard the gates of your mind.* Remember Paul's admonition in Philippians 4:8: "Whatsoever things are true … honest … just … pure … lovely … of good report … think on these things." When an unkind or impure thought enters your mind, *deal with it instantly.* If you cultivate it, it will take root and grow—and rob you of your joy. Sometimes Satan will throw his "fiery darts" at you, and sometimes he will use other people to do it for him. One of the best ways to defeat the wrong kinds of thoughts is to fill your mind with Scripture; so take time to memorize the Word of God.

6. *Remember that your joy is not meant to be a selfish thing; it is God's way of glorifying Christ and helping others through you.* Jesus first, Others second, Yourself last, and the result is JOY.

QUESTIONS FOR PERSONAL REFLECTION
OR GROUP DISCUSSION

1. What does it mean to be a "living sacrifice" to God?

2. What does it mean to be "transformed by the renewing of your mind"? How can this be accomplished?

3. Why is daily systematic reading of the Bible a must if you want joy and victory in your Christian life?

4. How can beginning the day with prayer prepare us for a joy-filled day in the Lord?

5. How will asking God to give you a submissive mind help you in your contacts with people each day?

6. How will being single-minded each day prepare us for difficult experiences we may have to face?

7. Why should we stop and take inventory of our state of mind and heart if we begin to lose our peace or joy during the day?

8. How can 1 John 1:9 help us maintain our joy throughout the day?

9. What should we do if we find wrong or impure thoughts creeping into our minds?

10. What have you learned from this study of Philippians that you feel will make a real difference in your Christian life?

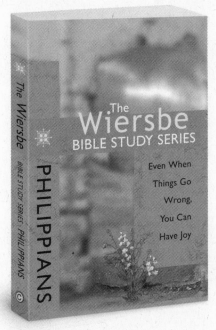

The "BE" series . . .

For years pastors and lay leaders have embraced Warren W. Wiersbe's very accessible commentary of the Bible through the individual "BE" series. Through the work of David C. Cook Global Mission, the "BE" series is part of a library of books made available to indigenous Christian workers. These are men and women who are called by God to grow the kingdom through their work with the local church worldwide. Here are a few of their remarks as to how Dr. Wiersbe's writings have benefited their ministry.

"Most Christian books I see are priced too high for me . . .
I received a collection that included 12 Wiersbe
commentaries a few months ago and I have
read every one of them.
I use them for my personal devotions every day and they
are incredibly helpful for preparing sermons.
The contribution David C. Cook is making to the
church in India is amazing."
—Pastor E. M. Abraham, Hyderabad, India